Uprooting *ANGER*: Eliminating the Emotion that Kills

CHARLES C. CUMMINS, MS, LPC

For more information or to purchase additional copies, contact:
Life Transitions Consulting Inc.
360 Chaffin Ridge Court
Roswell, GA 30075
Charlie@CharlieCummins.com
www.charliecummins.com

ISBN: 978-0-615-27923-7

Printed in the United States.

For Sandra and Christine

*Thank you for your unwavering love
and support.*

This symbol is called the Triratana, or Triple Gem, which is revered as a primary source of Buddhist teachings. The Triratana is made up of the three "priceless gems" of Buddha, Dharma and Sangha. Buddha is the first gem because he showed a way to end human suffering. Dharma, the second gem, represents the teachings of Buddha and the "way" of easing the suffering of others. The third gem of Sangha represents the teachers who have gone before us who pass down the teachings of Dharma.

Uprooting anger is an approach that emphasizes a philosophy of not contributing to the suffering of others. This book represents teachings both Western and Eastern teachings that have been passed down to me and that I now share with you.

What Clients Say about Charlie:

Charlie has exceptional skills in communicating with people and in motivating change. He is experienced, honest and passionate about working with others to enhance their lives.

> —*Michael D. Banov, MD, President*
> *Northwest Behavioral Medicine*

Charlie amazingly transforms people and excites them about making changes in their lives. He fills the room with energy and optimism while presenting an action plan of how to find success. He has a passion for life and for doing the work he loves.

> —*Sabrina Beck, MS, LPC*
> *Ridgeview Institute*

Charlie is a dynamic communicator with the ability to deliver material in a way that is entertaining and memorable. He introduces strategies that can be easily implemented to enhance human performance.

> —*Vanessa Lowry, President*
> *Profits in Progress*

My best one-word description of Charlie Cummins is *commitment*. Once Charlie commits to you and your company, you've got him—100% of him. Whether with his knowledge, experience or wisdom, Charlie doesn't hold back. I don't believe the man would know how to be a "partial participant." Charlie is a true professional.

> —*Donn Lowery, President/Owner*
> *Gould Electric Incorporated*

Table of Contents

A man is a bundle of relations, a knot of roots,
whose flower and fruitage is the world.
—Ralph W. Emerson

Introduction

What's begun in anger ends in shame.
—Ben Franklin

Anger has a poisonous effect on all our lives. On a personal level—in our families, work, communities, nation and world—anger permeates each of us. Anger creates distance away from people and generates a line of movement toward isolation and illness. It fractures leadership, feeds inefficiency, creates unhealthy alliances, and makes us sick.

Our world is shadowed by images of anger and examples of how one person's anger can have a ripple effect across the globe. With the efficiency of a Swiss watch, technology can inundate us with a flood of cheap, easy-to-access hatred, judgment, violence and indifference. Anger may even kill us one way or another, because it's like a poison that we can either sip, gulp or (hopefully) choose to reject.

Uprooting Anger is a guide to help you manage anger and work toward uprooting it and its related destructive emotions. If your fuse is short, your aggression high, your criticism sharp, your blaming personal, and your road rage unpublishable, this book is written for you.

If you just get angry when things don't go right, this book is also for you. Anger can rise to the surface of anyone's life and it does not discriminate based on age, race, gender, socioeconomic class or religion. Rather than focusing on merely managing anger, our goal is to completely uproot it and work toward its elimination.

For the last 25 years, I have struggled to manage my own anger and the anger my clients bring to the table. My work as a counselor, clinician, coach and

1 "

speaker in the field of clinical and humanistic psychology has laid a foundation for focusing on anger and destructive emotions. As a student of the martial arts, along with Buddhist and Asian studies, I have incorporated a great deal of this wisdom into my work with clients and their anger. I am devoted to improving human performance and life by working with business leaders, athletes, students and everyday individuals who struggle with issues of anger. It is through these experiences of personal growth, education, and practice in clinical psychology and Eastern studies that I weave together the approaches to managing anger in this book.

I believe the uprooting of anger is a summit that can be climbed. The theory, exercises and practices in this book were developed over years of working hand in hand with thousands of clients. I have learned to keep it simple, and have distilled both a philosophy and a host of tools that can produce profound life change.

Thousands of "techniques" are helpful in managing anger, but our goal is loftier. Still, to uproot anger, you need to put what you learn into practice, even though you may not master, or even learn to be comfortable with, all the strategies in this book. Seize this opportunity. Although it is important to manage your family and livelihood, don't obsess on that alone. Think of your future and the future of those you love and make a decision to change.

Regardless of your path or the techniques that work for you, your journey will produce results. Everybody's origin and circumstances of anger are different; that's what makes us individuals. Therefore, everyone's approach to eliminating anger will also be different. The most important thing is to develop a strong foundation of knowledge and understanding that you can build on. If your foundation is made of sand, your balance and longevity will suffer. Build a foundation of rock and move forward today.

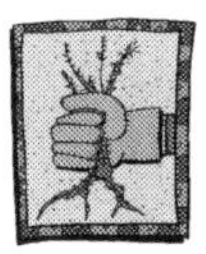

Chapter 1:
Understanding Anger

Although the world is full of suffering, it is full also of the overcoming of it.   *—Helen Keller*

Winters in Minnesota are frigid and, as I tell my daughter in my best fatherly voice, I often walked a mile to school on the snowiest of days. I didn't mind the walk because I was fortunate to live in an older neighborhood with gorgeous elm trees lining the street. In the summer, the trees created a cathedral of green down the avenue, and in the winter, a tent of white snow. In elementary school, I was a big boy with nicknames like "Chubby Charlie" and "Tank." All my pants were purchased from the "Husky" rack and needed to be hemmed by my grandmother before fitting correctly.

The walk to and from school was not so bad, but in third grade I began to take a different route. Instead of walking along the sidewalks of tree-lined Goodrich Avenue, I began to walk through the alleys of our neighborhood. The bullying and teasing from other boys about my size had driven me into hiding and led me to skulk my way between school and home. I traded my tree-lined walk for a perceived tunnel of safety down a garage-ladened corridor. At the age of eight, I could not have known how my path would give rise to my first and most indelible lessons about anger.

There is a strategy for walking and not being seen. To do this properly, I had to slink through the alleys and be willing to hide behind garbage cans, shrink to the size of telephone poles, and run in between garages. The greatest challenge, however, was to cross the streets at the end of each block without being seen. Unfortunately, being the size I was, I wasn't very fast and could be easily spotted by those patrolling the open routes of the neighborhood. On one particular winter's afternoon, I was sprinting across Victoria Avenue when the enemy spied me! As I huffed toward the alley on the other side, I heard it: "Chunky Charlie!" And then SPLAT! I had been hit with the icy sting of a snowball crashing against my head. (Please note that bullies often have good throwing arms; I was hit with a perfect strike from some distance.) Beneath the pain, anger shot through me in an instant. I remember the hurt and the heat as my temper grew and exploded into a foul-mouthed verbal tirade that may still echo throughout St. Paul. I was angry! I cried, but I was very angry.

Once word leaked back to my mother, courtesy of my sister, about the language I had used, I had bigger things to worry about—like my parents' anger and the punishment they would impose. They completely missed the issue of my being teased and clobbered in the head by a snowball! The chain reaction of my anger had been put into motion and the underlying issue forgotten.

Later that spring I was cornered again, this time on Avon Avenue by a sixth-grade redheaded bully. (Why is it that so many bullies have red hair?) But this day would have a different ending. As I was about to be pummeled, bouncing down the street came the most unlikely of heroes. Tommy Krakowski was an older boy who had taken swim lessons at our house the previous summer. He was very heavy and his body undulated as he ran to my rescue, picked up a fallen branch, and began to whip the tar out of my redheaded tormentor. Tommy was mentally slow, raised pigeons, and had likely faced his fair share of being teased, but he had a sense of right and wrong. Tommy knew about the hurt of being bullied by others and he also knew about anger. He taught me a great lesson that day because, although he had gotten angry, he did so out of compassion for me.

It was soon after this last incident when my father decided I needed help. The next Saturday, I was enrolled in the youth boxing league at the St. Paul Athletic Club. My dad was a smart and tough-minded attorney. He had been an athlete and flown for the Flying Tigers in China during World War II.

By the time Dad enrolled me, I had already developed an interest in sports and had played a season of park football. I didn't move well, but I didn't mind physical contact. After all, I was the biggest kid in the class and was put right in the middle of the offensive and defensive lines in football. My boxing coach was Jim Beattie, a former professional boxer who stood 6' 8.5" and was nicknamed The Skyscraper.

During practice, Mr. Beattie would tower over us while sparing from his knees. This was my introduction to boxing and my first lesson about anger: *Meet anger with greater anger and meet force with greater force.* As you will see, this lesson was somewhat misguided (or perhaps just misunderstood by me).

The Nature of Anger

To move beyond anger, you must first develop an understanding of anger. Although it relates to the body, and certainly affects the body, anger is primarily a mental factor of not being able to bear a person, object, situation or idea. Anger is frequently accompanied by a feeling of ill will or a desire to do harm. Anger is the most destructive emotion we have and is the result of deluded thinking, hatred, attachment and lack of understanding.

Throughout this book, I will refer to anger and destructive emotions in the same context, because anger includes a range of emotions including frustration, hatred, resentment, belligerence, annoyance and rage.

One of the most important lessons about the nature of anger is that destructive emotions are primarily based on false projections of the mind. All destructive emotions cause "obscured" or "afflictive" mental processes that prevent the mind from seeing reality as it is. With destructive emotions, as with emotional illness, there will always be a gap between the way things appear and the way things truly are.

Anger is parasitic and, once attached to our lives, it feeds off our physical, emotional and spiritual energy without giving anything in return. Not surprisingly, when we direct anger at others, those people will then be infected with anger. They too will be drained, receive nothing in return, and pass it on. Unless the anger is curtailed, it will get passed along to our loved ones, coworkers, the dog, drivers on the interstate, another country, or whatever we choose to punch, kick, scream at or cuss. Once unleashed, anger will spread like rings in a pond and infect everyone in its path.

Not only does the anger we unleash spread to others, but the more we are exposed to it, the more it takes root in our own lives. If you were raised in a household where anger was prevalent, the roots of your anger have likely grown deep. Bearing witness to anger in our culture and communities can tend to stimulate the root growth of anger. Constant exposure to images of anger through television and video games desensitizes us to anger and violence, which allows the root system of anger to spread more freely.

With each outburst, you rehearse its cycle and get better at it. The more you scream, criticize, journal, blog and strike out with anger, the more ingrained you make the habit. There are people who are champions at anger and its resulting insanity. These people have worked hard and suffered for their craft. These professionals of anger are easy to spot because they leave a trail of lost relationships, holes in walls and poor life decisions. The path of these anger professionals is frequently littered with legal troubles, hangovers and piles of regret.

Anger not only affects our present life, but may also disturb the past and the future. There is a tendency to hold onto the past episodes of anger in our relationships and, at some level, we always remember the times we've been hurt. If you believe in karma, cyclical existence, heaven and hell, or the belief that what goes around comes around, you understand that waves of anger can reach into our future and beyond.

Our Manic Society and Anger

As Americans, we are predisposed to higher degrees of stress and anger. Never before in the history of man has a society enjoyed such wealth and witnessed such monumental ambition. Americans work longer hours, take fewer vacations, give less time to their families, and accumulate more debt than any other culture in the world. We have grown into a society with great appeal and incredible technology, which has unleashed an unbridled brand of capitalism on the world. More and more, we have smaller families living in larger houses, we cultivate deep pools of wealth and shallow relationships, and we focus on material possessions and lose sight of our values.

At social gatherings, we frequently converse about what it was like when we were children and life seemed simpler and safer. It wasn't that long ago. Our culture has changed at a jack rabbit's pace, leaving us with a society that is impatient, craving, and slowly eroding the foundations of our community.

Modernization and the rapid advancement of technology have exceeded our ability as humans to evolve along with it, leaving us stressed, overwhelmed and increasingly angry. In the last 100 years, we have nearly doubled our life expectancy, yet rates of cancer, heart disease, diabetes, obesity, depression, anxiety, rage, violence and a host of other physical and emotional disorders continue to climb. As a society, we have reached the point where high levels of stress and anger seem unavoidable.

It's in Our Roots

In his book, *American Mania: When More Is Not Enough*, John Whybrow discusses how Americans are set apart from the world in a special way and how we were founded by a certain type of people.

The eighteenth century's "age of enlightenment" provided a framework for adventurous Europeans to colonize America in their own self-interest, with the goal of greater opportunity, freedom, capitalistic enterprise and republicanism. Whybrow details how we as a culture are uniquely driven by this migrant mindset. He explains that our ancestors were curious and had great resolve. They were ingenious risk takers with a love of competition and a belief in capitalism. Chinese and African-American populations, brought to this country as labor, also had tremendous resilience, resolve, and the universally human trait of curiosity. Our country is founded on the opportunity it represents for all people who are strong enough, shrewd enough and ambitious enough to survive and succeed.

In American ideology, the greatest failure is not viewed as failing itself, but rather as not picking yourself up and continuing the fight. As a society, we can be forgiving of failure, so we continue to risk it. We rejoice in victory and root for the underdog. As a society, our identity is linked to our love of competition that, as we will see, reinforces our self-interest and ever-growing free-market economy. As a population, we represent the largest single collection of such individuals in the world. This predisposition is not only inherent in our society, but may also have a genetic component.

It has long been speculated and supported in studies on primates that temperament, social behavior and impulsive aggressiveness have a genetic basis. Genetic links between temperament and novelty-seeking behaviors, such as extreme sports, have been researched by Ernest Noble, the Pike Professor of Alcohol Studies at the University of California Los Angeles. Noble has found a significant association between the presence of dopamine receptor alleles (D4-7) in the brain and "novelty-seeking behavior." People who possess the D4-7 allele are more likely to exhibit the curiosity-seeking and risk-taking behaviors possessed by our pioneering forefathers and in migratory populations throughout the world.

Dr. Chauseng Chen, in the School of Social Ecology at the University of California, Irvine, has analyzed available genetic data, specifically the D4-7 allele, along the major routes of ancient migration throughout the world. Dr. Chen's research supports the increased presence of the D4-7 allele in migratory populations and lower indicators of the D4-7 allele in less exploratory cultures. Conversely, in more stable and conservative cultures such as Japan, there are extremely low levels of the D4-7 allele throughout the population. In some areas of Asia, the allele does not even seem to exist! On the other hand, Americans, whose ancestors crossed the Bering Straits and the Atlantic, possess a preponderance of it.

What I'm saying is that we Americans, due to our inherent temperament and genetic predisposition, are a culture more inclined toward restlessness and risk taking. We are a population founded on capitalistic principles and individual freedom. Increasingly, we gauge our success on material gain, productivity and victories along the way. Simply put, our society is uniquely predisposed to higher levels of risk taking and stress and its natural result: anger.

Modernization

Although Americans live in a world of abundant choice and superheated technological advancement, we are paying an ever-increasing price. America has a paradoxical relationship with its prosperity; we see many families who have increased their disposable income yet are too busy to enjoy it. We often invest more in our earning and less in our families and social involvement within our community. As a society, parents and their children are chronically sleep-deprived because our increased goal-orientation demands supercharged routines and scheduled activities. When families recharge themselves, it is often linked to a computer, Blackberry or television...and less often with each other.

To accommodate this rapid pace, we have developed and named food and resources to fit our need: fast food, 24/7 service, online banking, Quick-Trip gas. We can TiVo our television and wire it to our computers so our employers and clients can access us at any time, and technology and the marketplace get the maximum commercial exposure from each moment in our lives.

As our daily lives continue to spin at an increasing rate, we are learning some disturbing facts about human nature. In times of material affluence, we struggle to set limits on our instinctual craving: when our desire for food, stimulation and material possessions are no longer constrained by limited resources, we will want more. Additionally, unchecked consumption erodes self-constraint and fosters a social malaise that only feeds our overindulgence and greed. In other words, we do not have a set point that tells us we've had enough.

As humans, we have an amazing capacity to do

without and to survive on very little. This is not true on the upper end of the extreme. Given an abundance of cheap food at a low cost, we will indulge. Given unlimited channels to surf, we will switch back and forth. With an abundance of income, we will spend more and take greater risks to get more. As we continue to indulge, we will experience a line of movement away from social interest and toward desire, overindulgence and greed.

Evidence of this paradigm has come full circle in the last year; capitalism seems to have reached a point of exhaustion. In 2008, we witnessed world governments struggle to arrest a global deflationary spiral in the form of a financial crisis that has never been seen before. The damage is so great that no expert can fully grasp the degree of damage that past decisions have had. Our financial collapse can be traced to four basic ingredients that directly reflect the fate of unchecked consumption discussed above.

1. The desire for more has led to massive leveraging by anyone and everyone. From consumers who bought houses they couldn't afford to hedge funds that bet three times their worth in cash.

2. The world economy is more intertwined than people realized and the failed American economy has unraveled global economy.

3. Globally entangled financial institutions have become so complex and singularly focused on profit that few CEOs dealing with them understand how they work.

4. This financial mess started right here in America with our toxic and greed-driven mortgage lending.

When a financial crisis starts in Greece, most countries can ride the wave and protect themselves. But when the crisis starts in America, no one can hide or find refuge. Combine our overheated capitalistic strivings with overly complex financial products, toss in too much leverage and global enmeshment, and we have a poisonous mix that is uniquely rooted in American culture.

Pandora's Box

All this might portray a bleak picture of Western society, capitalization, modernization and the predisposition toward stress that results in greater anger. However, it is what it is. Technology will continue to advance and our free-market economy will continue to bombard us with messages of temptation. Our companies will still demand access to us at all times, and traffic is not going to suddenly unclog. We have responded to the whispers from Pandora's Box, opened the lid, and released all the sorrows and vices of humanity. Life is stressful and we suffer for it. The good news is that all of us are resilient and have the seeds of love and compassion. We can uproot anger and the added suffering it stirs into the cup of life.

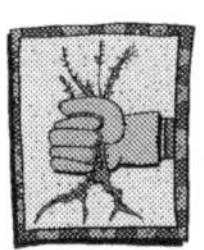 Chapter 2: The Facts about Anger

If you do not wish to be prone to anger, do not feed the habit; give it nothing which may tend to its increase.
—Epictetus

Boxing went well at the Athletic Club and it introduced me to other sports and general fitness. I swam on the swim team, wrestled, and gained self-confidence. Confidence is a tricky thing. You may feel it building inside even though it is somewhat unfamiliar and no one can quite see it. Sometimes it will continue to grow and slowly emerge on the surface like a plant sprouting its first leaves. And sometimes it fails to thrive at all. But sometimes confidence just needs a push.

That's what I got in the late spring of 1970 when the redheaded bully decided to seek his revenge for the tree limb he was force fed by Tommy Krakowski. (Bullies also have long memories and cronies who will dutifully carry out their bidding.)

I had just left the playground area on my Schwinn Orange Crate bicycle. As I turned up Linwood Avenue, my nemesis and his two goons pulled their bikes in my path. As they began to threaten me and describe the pounding I was about to receive, I had that feeling again: the heat was rising throughout my body. Only this time, instead of shouting profanity or freezing like a statue, my right foot shot out almost uncontrollably and kicked goon #1's bike! As he was straddling his bike, he fell over into the redhead, who fell into goon #2. Holy smokes! Before my very eyes was a tangle of bullies and their bikes all struggling to get up and hoping no one saw their disgrace! The kids still on the playground exploded in excitement as I quickly mounted my trusted Orange Crate and rode to the hills!

I recall few incidences of being bullied after that day. Plenty of teasing, but little bullying. Rumors spread about how I had taken out three older bullies and the legend kind of grew. My reputation as a pretty good boxer was also part of the myth. Sometimes you absolutely have to defend yourself, and sometimes you just have to face your fear. I was beginning to learn about anger and understand the difference between hurting others with anger and defending against it.

Anger and the Body

When you are angry and destructive, thoughts begin to percolate in your brain, specifically in the right prefrontal cortex (behind your right eyebrow). They produce a signal that stimulates the hypothalamus deep beneath the brain. The hypothalamic cells then reach farther down to the base of the brain through nerve cells, and eventually stimulate the adrenal glands. The adrenal glands then stimulate your kidneys, which pump adrenaline and cortisol into your bloodstream. Your body has kicked in its fight or flight response and is preparing for emergency action.

As anger grows, the adrenaline in your bloodstream increases your heart rate and raises your blood pressure. Your body temperature begins to rise as the adrenaline opens the arteries to your muscles. Next, your sympathetic nervous system constricts blood flow to your skin and internal organs as you begin to feel warm and experience a cold sweat at the same time. Your increased adrenaline levels now have blood surging through your body at a far faster rate than is healthy.

Cortisol and adrenaline are both associated with fat cell levels, which are now being dumped into your blood stream for energy. Eventually, your liver will convert this fat into cholesterol, which will produce clumpy, lumpy blood platelets and macrophages that begin to clog your arteries. Because your body thinks it's in a state of emergency, tiny subcellular clotting elements are also released into your bloodstream, only to find no open wound to be clotted! There is nowhere else for these clotting agents to go, so they remain in your already-thickening arteries.

We do have a parasympathetic nervous system that is responsible for calming the body, but the hypothalamus shut that off while you were angry. So your body begins to feel like it is in real danger as your heart pounds, your palms sweat, and your breathing becomes short and rapid. Your concentration becomes impaired, your impulse control is shot, and you are now raging with anger.

You have just tricked your body into thinking it was in eminent danger, wounded or under attack. Each time you get angry, your body experiences the same reaction. Every time you explode, you damage your body and shorten your life. Individuals who struggle to manage their anger are three times more likely to experience coronary heart disease. Every episode of anger suppresses the immune system, making you more vulnerable to illness and less able to heal. This is why anger is not on par with other emotions.

Anger and the Brain

State-of-the-art scientific methods for studying the brain have greatly increased our understanding of neurology and its link to emotions. Leading the research on the brain and emotion is Richard Davidson, head of a laboratory for affective neuroscience at the University of Wisconsin, Madison. Davidson's research provides the clearest picture of what areas of the brain are involved in emotion and in the regulation of emotions. To understand anger and destructive emotions, it is important to understand the mechanisms involved.

Just as there is no central hard drive for the brain, there is no central location for emotion. Davidson has found that the critical area of the brain involved in regulating emotion is the frontal lobe located behind the forehead. The human brain, as with all vertebrate species, is divided into left and right hemispheres. Left and right frontal lobes differ in their regulation of emotion. The left frontal cortex of the brain plays a primary role in positive emotions, while the right frontal lobe plays a primary role in negative emotions. Therefore, when we experience anger and destructive emotions, we have more brain activity in the right frontal lobe. The experience of positive emotions will provoke more brain activity in the left frontal lobe.

Another area of the brain involved in emotion is the parietal lobe, located behind the frontal lobe. Like the frontal lobe, it occupies two hemispheres. One detects sensation and the other is concerned with integrating sensory input. For our discussion, the parietal lobe provides us with a mental representation or "mind's eye" representation of our senses. Damage to the parietal lobe can affect our perception, our self-care, and certain aspects of our personality and memory.

The third area of the brain involved in emotion is the amygdala, which is part of the limbic system. The amygdala is an almond-shaped set of neurons located deep in the brain's temporal lobe. The amygdala has two parts located on either side of the brain. This part of the brain is important to regulation of emotions, and is particularly associated with fear and anxiety—helping us detect them and giving us ways to express them. It plays an important part in our "general-purpose defense" and reacts to unpleasant sights, sensations or smells. Anger, avoidance and defensiveness are largely controlled by the amygdala. Poor amygdalic functioning is associated with anxiety, autism, depression, post-traumatic stress disorder, phobias and schizophrenia. Impaired functioning will also result in an inability to detect environmental cues that would normally evoke fear and anxiety and to inhibit the expression of these emotions. The amygdala's size is directly correlated to the level of aggression in any given species, and humans with a history of aggression have been found to have an enlarged amygdala. On the opposite end, studies have shown that a shrinking of the amygdala is related to depression and memory loss.

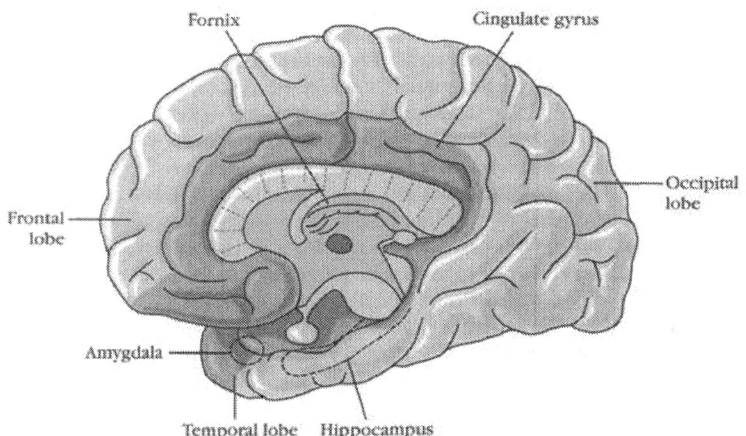

The hippocampus is a long structure, shaped somewhat like a seahorse, located just behind the amygdala. The hippocampus is responsible for encoding long-term memories and spatial navigation. It plays an important role in emotion because it is essential for our appreciation of the context of events. We often get this emotion when we walk into an environment.

After returning home from a vacation, we most likely feel a warm sense of security. When we walk into a new and unfamiliar social situation, we may feel uneasy or anxious. Abnormalities in the hippocampus are particularly linked to depression and post-traumatic stress disorder, which gives us a clearer view of why people with depression frequently experience sadness in situations that are not appropriate and show the slight shift in perception that is experienced in mental illness as well as anger.

Like the amygdala, the hippocampus shows a great deal of plasticity; it may shrink or become enlarged. In depression, for example, the hippocampus shows a measurable amount of shrinkage, which affects an individual's perception and desire to be in social settings. When depression is treated and overcome, the hippocampus returns to its normal size. An enlarged hippocampus has been associated with autism. In many cases, a depressed hippocampus causes an enhanced ability for remembering episodes from the past, but creates a struggle to relate or express this to others.

A simple diagnostic tool used in clinical settings is to evaluate whether an individual's emotions are congruent with the general context of their lives. If someone is angry while everyone else is experiencing a moment of joy, it can be assumed from a neurological perspective that they may have some dysfunction in the hippocampus. If this is the case, we know that it can be changed and that the hippocampus can return to its normal size.

Neuroplasticity

As we have just learned, the frontal lobes, the amygdala and the hippocampus change size in response to experience. Neuroplasticity is the brain's ability to reorganize itself by forming new neural connections—it changes, adapts, flows and regenerates itself. New neurons are constantly forming from stem cells, which have an amazing capacity to become any specific cell anywhere in the body. If one hemisphere of the brain becomes damaged, the healthy hemisphere will take over some of its functions. The brain can also change through experience and conditioning, as you will see later in this book when we discuss the negative thoughts that feed anger. The brain is malleable and, if we can transform the mind, we can transform the brain. If we can transform the brain, we can transform the body: "curus personalis," cure the whole person.

The Disadvantages of Anger

The parasitic nature of anger undermines our happiness and that of others. In addition to the obvious physiological and neurological effects of anger discussed above, there are many other disadvantages. Since anger is primarily a mental construct, it is important to understand the many ways in which anger distorts our perceptions of reality. Varied degrees of distorted perception are also characteristic of mental illnesses such as depression, anxiety, addiction and psychosis.

By its very nature, anger sees and projects only negative qualities. In anger, there is a tendency to exaggerate and superimpose our negativity, yet we can't see that we are doing so. While angry, we believe that our thinking is right, yet our physical and emotional response clearly indicates that it is not. The angry mind seems clear that it is right and others are wrong and should change. Anger generates black-and-white thinking, with no room for negotiation. It increases blame and breeds suspicion.

Anger pushes people away, creates isolation and promotes unhappiness. Generally, the first people pushed away are those closest to us. We push them away by criticism, suspicion and continual unhappiness. When angry, we struggle in our ability to communicate and express ourselves. We rage and shun people while fermenting bitterness and resentment. We lose our compassion for the suffering of others and become selfish. Anger also creates a "refractory period" that, for a time, closes us off from advice or anything that contradicts our view.

Anger is a symptom of several mental disorders, including depression and addictions. When infected with anger, we are, in that moment, insane. But what is most insane is that expressing our anger, while perhaps temporarily making us feel better, doesn't get rid of it. If it did, we wouldn't get so angry again, and again and again. Practicing anger only makes us better at it.

The Benefits of Anger

We have now seen why anger is considered the most destructive of all emotions, but it is important to gain a balanced perspective of anger and review its few benefits. First, anger can be useful in self-protection. It can arouse our bodies into a state where we can act with maximum force in response to potential harm. Second, anger can serve the purpose of decompression, where our bodies are given a chance to release pent-up physical tension caused by too much frustration. This cathartic release often produces the "calm after the storm" effect of relaxing our nervous system, which can return us to balance. Developing a safe, physical outlet for this energy will be discussed later, because routine expressions of aggression will only produce more episodes of aggression.

Lastly, anger can be an excellent motivation for overcoming an obstacle or achieving a goal in life. In fact, the devastation anger has caused can be used as the primary motivator to eliminate patterns of anger from our lives.

Beginning the Journey

Reflect for a moment on how you have begun your search for greater peace and the ability to manage your anger. What efforts have you taken along this path and why? I went through my stages of rebellion and plunged myself into the human-potential movement. I've explored many faiths, read a library of self-help books, and attended countless workshops. I have practiced martial arts, thrown my butt out of a plane more than a thousand times (honest!), and meditated in caves. But something always remained missing and my inner conflict remained.

Despite our efforts, most people are at war with themselves and other people in some way or another. We run through the week in competition with others and our imaginary foes. Our days are filled with confrontation and mounting frustration, while being driven by the fear that we are somehow "not good enough." We live in the world's richest nation, yet are chronically insecure and defensive while facing a constant flood of crisis and conflict pumped out by the attention-grabbing media.

Instead of waiting for the magic bullet, uprooting anger is about taking responsibility for your life and conquering your anger through insight and action. Through a shift in attitude and thought, you can create greater peace in yourself and those around you right now. By understanding the big picture of anger and the larger patterns of life, you can take action and move beyond competition to cooperation. You can learn how to become the antidote, not the catalyst, to your suffering and the suffering of others.

Personal Exercise: Self-Assessment

Let's begin the journey by identifying the areas of your life where you are not at peace. Do these statements sound familiar? Highlight the ones that do and feel free to add your own:

❏ *I am not at peace with my body.* It feels sluggish and fat, keeps me awake at night, craves alcohol, aches, limps, belches, wheezes, feels weak and gets into accidents.

❑ *I am not at peace with my career.* It is too stressful, too far away, and filled with tension and disappointment. I am surrounded by negative people, impossible deadlines and insecurity. I am angry, trapped, kept down, exhausted and fearful.

❑ *I am not a peace with my relationships.* I feel angry, disappointed, fearful, insecure, trapped, dominated, manipulated, misunderstood, taken for granted and resentful. I can't seem to communicate honestly and effectively with the people I care about.

❑ *I am not at peace with my family.* I feel alone, bored, unloved, guilty, resentful, angry, trapped, restless, manipulated, overburdened and exhausted. I feel that I am losing myself in them.

❑ *I am not at peace with my finances.* I am afraid for my future and feel anxious, overwhelmed with debt and trapped. I struggle to pay my bills, I have accrued too much debt, and there is never enough money to do what I would like. I feel insufficient as a provider.

❑ *I am not at peace with myself.* I feel frustrated, lost and confused. There is too much conflict in my life and I seem to always be shouting to be heard. I often do things for others and never have time for myself. I don't accomplish as much as I would like, which leaves me feeling as if I am not good enough.

❑ *I am not at peace with my world.* All the bad news makes me feel nervous and anxious. I am losing trust in just about everyone and everything. I am depressed about the future and have lost my optimism. I am afraid that we are killing and overpopulating the planet and afraid of what we're leaving future generations. I alternate between being cynical and numb, and I feel powerless to make a difference.

❑ *Others:*

____

____

———————————————————————————————
———————————————————————————————
———————————————————————————————
———————————————————————————————
———————————————————————————————

By highlighting and writing out the areas where you are not at peace, you have begun to list opportunities for change and identify the areas of your life that are being affected. In a later chapter, you will be asked to assess your overall balance in life. Draw on the statements from this exercise when you begin to focus on specific change.

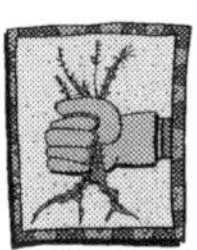 # Chapter 3: Extinguishing Anger's Energy

People have a hard time letting go of their suffering. Out of a fear of the unknown, they prefer suffering that is familiar   *—Thich Nhat Hanh*

Athletics and exercise can be an effective tool to help manage anger and release anger's energy. I learned this at an early age while boxing and playing football. These sports are violent, and it wasn't long before I realized that the harder I hit people, the louder the crowd would cheer. If I had a bad day or got teased, I always had an outlet when I walked onto the field or into the gym. Sports—violent sports in particular—can be a release and an aphrodisiac. It took a long time and a lot of hurt before I realized that athletics and exercise are good tools, but not enough to completely overcome anger.

Imagine your anger as a diseased tree growing within your life. If your anger is great, imagine your tree as a mighty oak with far-reaching branches and a deep root system. There are many strategies and techniques for managing anger that fall short because all they do is trim diseased branches from your anger tree. The tree, its roots, and its disease still remain. To uproot the anger tree, you must develop a philosophy that helps you dig deep beneath the roots. The ultimate goal is to uproot and eliminate the anger tree completely.

Movement

You can tell a lot about people by observing their movement in life. From their thoughts, expressions and behaviors, you can paint a picture of their goals, what kind of material they're made of, where they have been, and where they hope to be. As a therapist and coach, I learned a long time ago to listen to people's words but trust what they do and their line of movement. From people's movement you can discern their logic, morals, and the meaning they give to life. If there is incongruence between what people say and what they do, you can deduce that there is a struggle or an affliction in their life.

Movement is life, and lack of movement will lead us to death. Every illness, neurosis and affliction we experience has the same goal of trying to slow us down, create isolation, and keep us from moving forward. When we stop moving completely, we die. So creating movement in your life is the key to overcoming anger and illness. Life expresses itself in motion, and a person's line of movement will point the direction for future success or failure. You can read all the philosophies and strategies you want, but until you begin to apply them, you will experience little change.

Sometimes we are so slowed by affliction that only a little movement is possible. These episodes happen in people's lives, but there is always a little wiggle room to create motion in some manner. Movement doesn't always have to be big and may involve just tiny steps. Move too fast and you will run out of energy and fall short of your goals. Move too slow and the burdens of change may grind you to a halt. By reading these words, you are creating movement. With each step forward, you will make progress and advance the cause of uprooting your anger.

Social Interest

Alfred Adler coined the concept of social interest in 1911. Adler was a contemporary of Sigmund Freud until he broke away and formed his own psychological society, which he called individual psychology. Social interest, or *gemeinschaftsgefuhl* in German, is the most fundamental and most complex concept of individual psychology. Social interest reflects Adler's belief that everyone has the potential to be consciously developed and that cultivating a sense of social feeling, community sense, communal sense, and identification with humanity is the essential ingredient. Developing social interest is one of the few goals in life that can't be used on both the useful and useless sides of life. In fact, social interest is the primary direction of movement toward the useful side of life.

Movement toward the useless side of life is characterized by pessimism, self-absorption and goals of being superior to others. Movement on the useful side of life is characterized by courage, confidence, optimism and a sense of humor.

Adler described social interest as being an attitude to life that involves empathy with others, "to see with the eyes of another, to feel with the heart of another." It is through social interest that we develop a positive direction of movement in life and create a sense of belongingness with humankind and the universe.

You can't overcome anger by moving in a direction of isolation. To uproot anger, you have to practice, and you practice by increasing your social interest and interaction with others. Individuals with high degrees of social interest are healthier physically and emotionally throughout their lifespan.

The goal and line of movement of every physical and psychological disorder is to move you in a direction of isolation. Therefore, generating a line of movement toward social interest is mandatory and healthy. You may not always feel like reaching out, contributing or being around people, but social interest helps you create a firm foundation that you can build on to uproot anger.

Extroverts' personalities are more wired for high degrees of social interest than people who are shy or introverted. Some people may not be comfortable with their social skills so they avoid most social situations. Others may be hindered from developing social interest because of health reasons. The fact remains, however, that, despite our personality, skill variance, or limitations, we are all human beings. And, as human beings, our nature is to contribute and develop social interest within our world. We are born into families and arguably need more nurturing, security and care for a longer period than any other species. Humankind is not well equipped to deal with nature on its own. It has been true throughout history, and has never been truer than today. If we don't work together, we will all suffer greatly and put our existence in peril.

Like the concept of movement, developing social interest can be taken in tiny steps. Begin by reaching out to your family or those who support you. To interact with strangers, join a book club, attend a seminar, take a class on an area of interest, volunteer. Social interest is about connecting with other people and contributing, so make eye contact with others and engage in conversation. (Surfing the Internet, blogs, chat rooms, online gaming and text messaging are not active examples of social interest, but instead provide environments for isolation.) If you have pushed people away with your anger, make amends. You now have a positive direction of movement to focus on.

Let's now look at some additional reasons for cultivating social interest.

Suffering

My guess is that you have picked up this book for a reason. You have likely been fighting a battle in your head or in your life. You are hurt or have been hurting others, and are not sure what to do about it. Frustration and destructive emotions have fueled your anger, or you could be suffering from depression, anxiety, substance abuse, divorce, job loss or legal problems. Perhaps your relationships have suffered, you feel stuck, and you may be numb to how much suffering surrounds your life. Or you've been waging a war inside your head—a war of self-blame, blaming others, hurt and bewilderment about your own suffering. Maybe you have been the recipient of another's anger and you are confused about it.

It's an unavoidable fact: People suffer. At our moment of birth, there is suffering. Throughout our lives, there is suffering. At death, there is suffering. As a part of our existence, we will all lose someone or something we love. In our bodies, and through our emotions, we experience pain. We all experience a rainbow of afflictive emotions such as sadness, annoyance, fear, anxiety and anger. We've been teased on the playground or embarrassed by our actions. We create accidents and are involved in those created for us. We experience both intentional and unintentional harm.

As humans, we can both feel and create suffering like no other creature on the planet. We do not need physical pain to experience suffering, and we can take on the suffering of others. We will go to extremes to avoid or numb our pain, yet we have the unique capacity to create our own suffering through distorted thinking. Life will shoot arrows of suffering in our direction and we can create a thousand wounds in our mind. An approach to disciplining the mind and reducing this self-created suffering will be discussed in later chapters.

The Buddhist term for suffering is *dukkha* and the Buddhist philosophy of the Four Noble Truths provides an excellent framework for understanding suffering and finding your way out of it.

The Four Noble Truths

Dukkha: The truth of suffering.

Samudaya: The true cause of suffering.

Nirodha: The true cessation of suffering.

Magga: The true path to cessation of suffering.

Dukkha: The Truth of Suffering

To live means to suffer, because human nature isn't perfect and neither is the world we live in. In our lifetime, we will endure physical and emotional suffering, pain, sickness, injury, old age, psychological suffering and loss. There are different degrees of suffering and there are also positive experiences in life such as love and happiness, which are the opposite of suffering. Because all good things must end, we must understand that everything in life is impermanent. We will never be able to keep the things we desire and strive for in our lives. Sad times, and happy moments, will always pass by. We, and all we love, will pass one day too.

Samudaya: The True Cause of Suffering

The true cause of suffering is in our attachment to transient things, our desires, and the ignorance that arises from these two. Attachments to transient things include not only the material objects that surround us, but also ideas, faith, ourselves, and much of what we perceive. Desire and its ensuing suffering are generally reflected in three ways:

1. The desire and constant seeking of pleasure through the body or other senses.

2. The desire to become something other than what we are now through ambition or attainment.

3. The desire to get rid of things like suffering and anger.

Ignorance arises from a lack of understanding of how our attachment to impermanence generates increased suffering. Ignorance also refers to indifference toward these things and life in general.

Nirodha: **The True Cessation of Suffering**

The way out of suffering is to eliminate attachment and desire. The third noble truth expresses the idea that suffering can be ended by attaining dispassion for those things in life that we cling and attach ourselves to so dearly. This means that our suffering and the suffering of others can be overcome through nonattachment. This doesn't mean we don't love the things and relationships in our life, but that we need to understand that all things can and will pass.

Magga: **The True Path to Cessation of Suffering**

The path to the end of suffering is a gradual journey of self-improvement, described in Buddhist teachings as the eightfold path: right view, right intention, right speech, right action, right livelihood, right effort, right mindfulness and right concentration. In addition to the eightfold path, the fourth noble truth emphasizes the need to develop these qualities to the point of full mastery.

The whole aim of this Buddhist teaching is to begin developing the reflective mind in order to identify and overcome your own delusions. The Four Noble Truths is a teaching about letting go and asking yourself:

> Why is there suffering?

> What are the causes of suffering?

> Am I the cause of my own suffering or the suffering of others?

> Do I want to be the *cause* of suffering or the *antidote* to the suffering of others?

It's important to understand that the concepts of desire and attachment are not intended to prescribe a path of a Spartan, monastic life, but instead to serve as a reminder about how you want to live your life. There is nothing wrong with wanting a nice house or vehicles for your family, or wanting love, good health and beauty. It is good for us to take explorative vacations and invest in good education. The problem lies in becoming overly attached to these things and subtly failing to be mindful of their impermanence. With attachment, when we experience an inevitable loss, our suffering is somehow greater. We should also be aware of how our actions affect the attachment of others and how they too will suffer with a loss.

Problems arise when our desire dictates our emotions, thoughts and behaviors. Desire is a thirst that is never satisfied by money, possessions, sex, gambling, substances or thrills. Refreshing ourselves at the fountain of desire is like drinking sand; it will only facilitate our suffering and anger. What I believe we truly thirst for in life rests in the qualities of social interest, love and compassion.

The Positive Side of Suffering

Not all suffering is bad; certain aspects of suffering have positive attributes. People who never really experience suffering in their life may not develop the capacity to manage suffering and use the tools to get rid of it. Suffering can also be a powerful opponent to arrogance, pride, and feelings of superiority that can stifle the growth of other, more positive traits. When we face suffering in our lives and search for the causes, we learn that our negative thoughts contribute to this. In this sense, we can gain freedom from suffering and engage in more liberating thoughts and activities.

With the experience of suffering, we can recognize that other beings also suffer and are in pain. Through this understanding, we can develop compassion for others. The emergence of compassion for all sentient beings because of their suffering generates movement toward social interest. Increased social interest, love, compassionate thoughts and compassionate actions are fundamental tools to up-root anger.

While it is important to have an understanding of the nature of suffering, it is even more important to have some exercises to help us engage in better understanding this philosophy. These exercises help to cultivate an awareness of others' suffering and reinforce the mindset of helping ease the suffering of others.

Personal Exercise: Awareness of Suffering
Think about three people who are close to you and write down the suffering you have observed in their lives. If you can't come up with anything, ask them. That can be a healthy conversation for both sides and a great opportunity to listen and practice empathy.

Now reflect on the question of how you may be contributing to the suffering of others through your actions, inaction or words.

Now make a list of how you might be able to ease the suffering of these people. In some cases, you may find that you are powerless in this regard. This ineptitude frequently occurs when the problem is too big, too far away, or beyond our capabilities and resources. If this is the case, I find it helpful to pray for their well-being and easement of their suffering. I also vow that I will not add to their suffering. Sometimes that's all we can do.

Compassion

The most potent antidote to counter and prevent anger is love and compassion. While anger involves the desire to harm others, love and compassion are the heartfelt wish for other beings to have happiness and relief from their suffering. Love and compassion are natural to human beings, and are also the source of skills that can be developed and learned. True compassion comes from the heart and is not contrived, much like that of parents wanting to remove the suffering of their child.

Compassion is selfless and carries no expectation of something in return. We often extend a kindness, but are subtly offended when we don't receive a thank you or pat on the back. We need to let go of these expectations. Love, kindness and compassion are not only useful to us, but to the whole of human society, so extend your kindness and compassion without expectation and everyone benefits. Be a model for your children and everyone you come in contact with. Cultivating compassion is not just for those who practice religion; it is for everyone who considers themselves a part of the human family. Compassion is a form of spiritual democracy and recognizes that every human being has an equal right to have and cultivate happiness.

Owen Flanigan, a philosophy professor at Duke University, offers an interesting view on compassion and its role in society from a traditional Western philosophical perspective that breaks individual compassion down into three types:

Rational Egoists: These individuals primarily watch out for their own well-being, but see rationally that, to get what they want, they must be nice to others. Rational egoists are wise enough to understand that their own good depends on treating others well.

Selfish Compassionate: These individuals are primarily focused on taking care of their own needs.

Then, if there are time and resources left over, they will extend compassion to others.

Compassionate and Selfish: These individuals are primarily compassionate and loving, but if there is a scarcity of resources, such as food, water or shelter, their compassionate side will shed and their selfish side emerge.

Dr. Flanigan's perspective raises the question of compassion being purely altruistic. Can compassion apply to ourselves as well as to others? Aristotle said that self-love is not egotistical but it does involve respecting yourself. The Buddhist concept of compassion is the wish that "I may be free of suffering and free of the sources of suffering." With this understanding of compassion for ourselves, we can develop empathy and see the kinship in others and, in turn, feel compassion for others. Compassion for ourselves is not selfish—it is self-respect. When we battle issues of self-esteem or a lack of self-respect, we are in no position to extend compassion to others. Therefore, our goal is to cultivate compassion for both others and ourselves in an effort to uproot the tree of anger.

Compassion changes the brain in a positive way. Some of Richard Davidson's neuroscience research has specifically focused on the effects of compassion on the brain. What he has found is that perception and imagination are very closely linked. In this case, the mental practice of cultivating compassion through thought, prayer, meditation, mindfulness and other practices leads us to the actual acts of compassion toward others. This is another example of neuroplasticity and how we can shape our thoughts and, therefore, change our behavior.

Mental practice or rehearsal involves repeating a thought or mental image long enough to produce changes in the circuitry of the brain. This technique has been used throughout history in sports, the performing arts, and religious practices. Athletes and performers are frequently taught to visualize their actions, their route, their role and their opponent, and focus on the desired outcome. By mentally rehearsing their event, these individuals are better prepared to execute in competition and performance. Musicians who practice extensively have been shown to enhance the conductivity of the brain. The practice of meditation, as we will discuss in more depth later, improves the synchronicity of the brain and even thicken the cerebral cortex, resulting in improved concentration and memory.

Most importantly, Davidson has shown that thoughts and acts of compassion stimulate enhanced activity in the left frontal lobe of the brain that is associated with more positive emotions. In other words, if you want to combat the negative thinking associated with anger and affliction, which is associated with the right frontal lobe, begin to engage in compassionate thought and action.

It has also been shown that compassionate thoughts and actions raise serotonin levels in the brain. Serotonin is the neurochemical most closely associated with mood. In fact, compassionate acts toward others not only raise our serotonin level and the levels in the person we help, but the levels will also increase in anyone who witnesses our act of compassion. When we engage in selfless acts of kindness, we are the first person to benefit, but anyone who receives or witnesses our act of kindness also benefits personally and on a neurological level.

I have just presented a set of incredible tools to help you begin to not only manage your anger, but also begin working toward uprooting it. If you make a commitment to move in the direction of social interest and understand that you and all humans experience suffering, you are left with the choice of either contributing to continued suffering or being the antidote. In choosing to be the antidote, you must be mindful of suffering and its causes, while generating compassionate thoughts and actions toward other human beings. As you cultivate compassion within yourself, you are the first person who benefits because you are rewiring the circuitry of your brain and enhancing the activity in the brain associated with positive emotions. Through your practice of kindness, your brain will become less accustomed to destructive emotions and more familiar with positive ones. Your actions will become more positive and everyone you meet will benefit. You are now on the path to uprooting the tree of anger.

Sadness and Anger

Another way to reshape our understanding of anger is to view it from a perspective I have used in practice for years. I have learned that, in many cases, anger and sadness are the same emotion and differ only in what we do with them. This core emotion becomes anger when we project it outwardly, and becomes sadness when we hold it in. The path of dealing with either sadness or anger has its drawbacks, but sadness is a much easier emotion to work with and is more conducive to change.

By its very nature, anger pushes people away. We become angular and red in the face. Our voice deepens and becomes louder as our chest puffs up and our back straightens. Sometimes we clench our fists, our breathing changes, we cross our arms and generally close people off. Everything about anger says, "Get away from me." In anger, our thinking becomes irrational and narrow in focus. We are then truly insane—it's where the term "mad with anger" comes from. If you are trying to make sense of someone who is in a state of anger, you are wasting your time. If you think you can influence someone when they are in a rage, you are the more insane person.

Working with anger by focusing on the incidences of it will leave you frustrated. As a young therapist, I would dutifully attempt to help clients with their anger issues. A client would arrive for their session and proceed to tell me about an episode of anger that got out of control and I would thoughtfully work with them to resolve that particular issue. Next week, they would arrive for their session and tell me about a different episode, and we would work to find a solution for that episode and develop a plan of action. The following week, my client would arrive and inform me of yet another episode that was different from all prior weeks. Focusing on resolving specific incidences of anger left me feeling like the Dutch boy trying to plug leaks in a dam. As long as we continued to focus on resolving specific issues of anger, the cycle would continue and the client would continue to push people out of his life while making himself sick. There was little progress and, with each episode of anger, he only got better at it.

While anger pushes people away, sadness draws people together. As human beings, it is our nature to want to ease the suffering of others and, when we see someone or something that is sad, hurt or wounded, we intrinsically move toward that person in an effort to help. Beneath the frustrations of our life, the difficulties in relationships, the struggles with family, and the battles within us is sadness. If we can resolve the issues of sadness, we can undermine anger. Revealing our sadness brings people within our circle who can help, instead of pushing them away with anger and leaving us in isolation. Once again, by focusing on sadness, we are generating a healthier direction of movement toward social interest.

When approaching anger in this way, I should point out an issue of timing. To simply ignore a person's anger and attempt to cut straight to underlying issues of sadness may just create more aggravation. Many times episodes of anger are about being heard, and you must allow people this opportunity. However, when the person bleeds off some of their energy and the initial wave of adrenaline has passed, this is a good time to ask, "What about all this is making you sad?" or "This mess is really making me sad; how about you?" These simple statements of empathy and compassion have an amazing ability to uproot the anger and open the branches to a person's underlying sadness. As human beings, we are much more equipped to work together, solve the issues of sadness that arise, and take one more step toward uprooting your anger.

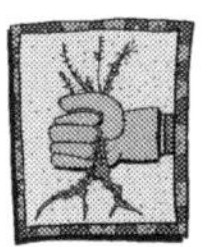# Chapter 4: The Mind, Emotion and Anger

A mind, like a home, is furnished by its owner, so if one's life is cold and bare, he can blame none but himself.
                                              —Louis L'Amour

As I completed elementary school, I was outgrowing my chubbiness and becoming focused on not just athletics, but *performance* in athletics. I put myself through the Charles Atlas course of fitness using "dynamic tension" exercises and his "clean" approach to life. I was always playing football, hockey, track and field or tennis. I was not a natural student or athlete, but was learning that I had the ability to create success. I knew I was going to have to work harder than most to achieve it. The summer between seventh and eighth grades, I spent two weeks canoeing and camping in the boundary waters of Canada. I spent the rest of my summer at my first job as a tool and lens grinder at Soderberg Optical and working out in a smelly weight room in the basement of St. Paul's downtown YMCA.

I trained under the supervision of 30-year-old Donny Whit, a hulk of a man and a Midwest champion power lifter. Donny took me under his very large wing, both at work and in the weight room at the Y. Donny became a teacher of weight training and a *sensei* of mental attitude. All he asked from me was to join him in that old basement and put forth my best effort. My memory of that place is similar to the bar scene in *Star Wars*, with a wild assortment of men from varied backgrounds who screamed, grunted and told boastful stories. You can learn a lot by simply observing life, and many of my lessons I learned by spending time with the characters in that room.

Donny taught me four things about weight training: bench press, squats, cleans and dead lift. He told me about the importance of proper technique and kept his approach to weight training simple. But most importantly, he taught me about putting forth maximum effort and consistency in life. If you do your best and strive for consistency in your thoughts and actions, you can accomplish great things—like uprooting anger.

I worked out with Donny every summer of high school. He would visit soy farms outside the Twin Cities and purchase huge bags of pure soy powder so I could gulp it down three times a day to build strength. Although very bad tasting, it was better than choking down raw eggs, as was popular after the first *Rocky* movie. Other kids had caught up to me in size and I was no longer the biggest kid on the field, but I was certainly one of the strongest. I had great success in the area of athletics, moderate success in the classroom, and struggled mightily with the adolescent battle over my mind, emotions and anger.

The first lessons I learned about the mind, emotions and anger were in high school, where adolescence itself becomes a food processor that constantly churns the thoughts and feelings that influence our behavior. For me, the product of this soup was frequently an explosion of anger that was often misdirected. If I was provoked, I would fight back. But sometimes I would rail against others even when not provoked. I would just manufacture conflict and fight against the demons of my own creation.

An old Chinese proverb refers to this pattern by stating something to the effect of "If you have no enemies within, no enemies outside of you can do you harm." In other words, our own inner demons frequently create unrest and lead us to fight a self-created war against the world. If we can learn to identify, understand and tame these inner demons, many of the outer battles we fight in life will cease to exist. Little did I know as an adolescent how my thoughts would dictate my emotions and behaviors and how we as humans differ from all other beings in relation to thinking and our ability to create our own suffering.

While the brain is made up of material matter, the "mind" is nonmaterial and refers to the thinking, perceptual, and experiential part of us. The mind is our body's hard drive that integrates our experiential learning through our senses and mental consciousness. The mind gives us the capacity to experience sounds, tastes, smells, touch and intuition. As we go through life, we experience many emotions, realizations and types of mind. We can have a joyful mind, a patient mind, a compassionate mind, and/or an angry mind.

The human mind can be both the source of great happiness and a source of great suffering, since all emotions can be enhanced or diminished at the mental level. Therefore, if your goal is to eliminate your anger, you must begin at the level of your mind and mental consciousness.

Unique to humans is not our ability to learn, but to derive what we learn from two directions. The first direction is being able to see an object, study it and gain knowledge. The second is our capacity to create a mental image of something. When you read the word "snow," what do you think about? You probably instinctively create an image of snow. Not only that, this image of snow may link to other related thoughts and images: cold, Minnesota, Vikings, football, fall, leaves, snowmen, sleds, etc. Many of us have lost sleep by trying to stop thinking of something by trying to stop thinking of something. It doesn't work.

With anxiety disorders, the trigger for an attack is not only related to a fearful situation, but can also be set off by fearful thoughts or projections of the mind that cause the fight or flight response. In many cases, our anger is also generated by distorted projections of someone or some place. The more you try to suppress or control these thoughts, the more likely they are to bounce back with greater strength. Negative thinking and angry thoughts are based on well-rehearsed patterns of rumination that we engage in both consciously and subconsciously. In most cases, these negative thought patterns serve the unhealthy purpose of avoiding or escaping problematic life situations. At the root of these problematic life situations is our own sadness or suffering, both real and perceived. The good news is, if we have the capacity to generate our own suffering, we also have the capacity to uproot it.

Self-created emotional suffering is greatly influenced by how we respond to a certain situation. If you overreact or become excessively sensitive, your frustration will only increase. When you take things personally or perceive life as unfair, you perpetuate a negative cycle that will lead you to believe that your problems are permanent. See no end to your suffering and resistance to change begins to set in. As resistance grows, your movement slows and anger and frustration begin to take root.

Individuals who struggle with their anger will often try to avoid situations or cues that might set them off. However, life has a funny way of challenging us with novel situations or triggers, and our anger usually finds a way to resurface. Avoidance, although it can separate us from provocative situations, is a poor tool for learning to manage our anger, and it teaches us nothing about coping with anger. The goal, then, is to learn how to remain peaceful in the face of violence and our own distorted thinking.

We begin by learning to understand and challenge our destructive patterns of thought. Great people such as His Holiness the Dalai Lama, Jesus, Mahatma Gandhi, and Martin Luther King, Jr. all faced incredible suffering in their lives but overcame their thoughts of anger to teach a philosophy of nonviolence. You can do this as well.

Because human beings have the unique capacity to self-create wounds through our thinking, it is important to extract these thoughts, view them, understand them, and rework them in order to change them. Fortunately, our irrational thoughts generally fall into certain categories of thinking. We will review these so you can begin to identify patterns you may have with distorted thinking.

Distorted Thought Patterns

All-or-nothing thinking. Things are either black or white, good or bad. If a situation falls short of being perfect, it's a total failure. To balance this, you must remember that a middle ground exists and few things in life are perfect. If you view everything short of perfect as a failure, how can you take joy in what is good?

Overgeneralization. You often conclude about something or someone based on one negative event or impression. Overgeneralization is easy to identify because it usually involves the words "always" or "never," such as "things never work out for me." This negative self-talk is a prescription for self-defeat.

Discounting the positive. You have difficulty accepting praise or enjoying the positive experiences in life. In this pattern, you may reject positive experiences as being rare and you are likely to minimize your own good work. Thus, discounting the positive will leave you feeling inadequate and unfulfilled even when things are going well.

Blaming. You hold other people or circumstances responsible for your suffering and ignore your self-created suffering. No one likes being someone else's scapegoat, and blaming quickly creates isolation.

Personalization. You see yourself as responsible for the suffering and happiness of everyone around you, even when you are not. Everything people say and do is some kind of reaction to you. Personalization is self-centered and generates a lot of guilt, shame and feelings of failure.

Should statements. I call this "shoulding on yourself," because you have ironclad rules about how things *should* be in your life. Should statements lead to frustration when things don't go your way and/or live up to your expectations.

Mental filtering. You tend to make the negative details of a situation the primary focus of your attention. These details frequently become blown out of proportion and all positive aspects are filtered out. Dwelling on the negative is symptomatic of a mental disorder and, when things continue to look much worse than they are, reality will eventually become distorted.

Being right. You feel that you must continually prove that you are right or correct, as if you are on trial. You are out to prove a point and being wrong is unthinkable. You are likely to go to great lengths to prove your point.

Mind reading. Without their saying so, you know what people are feeling and why they act the way they do. In particular, you are able to discern how people feel toward you. These assumptions often untrack communication and lead to interpersonal conflict.

Catastrophizing. You expect disaster, and "what if" statements keep you from experiencing things in life. This is most frequently emotional reasoning, not based on a realistic appraisal of the situation.

Like all illnesses, these distorted thought patterns have the line of movement toward negativity and isolation. These patterns tend to create distance between people and open the door to mental struggles. When we personalize, catastrophize, generalize, blame and *should* on ourselves, we rehearse patterns of thought that create a shade of isolation and distorted perception of reality. Like a cloud that slowly descends over our head, distorted thought patterns alter how we perceive events and how we take in information. Patterns of distorted thought and perception can also occur in other ways through what I call our own ego afflictions.

The Five Ego Afflictions

I believe that one of the reasons people enjoy being in the woods, at the beach, climbing a mountain, diving from a plane, or simply being outdoors is that there is so little ego conflict in nature. Time spent in nature is time not spent in a world of colliding egos. When we escape from media messages, jockeying for positions in traffic, etc., there is space to see ourselves for who we really are. Too often, we spend our lives wrapped up in "my time," "my money," "my space" and "my people."

As a society, we are increasingly attached to the "I-ness" of who we are: "I deserve," "I want," "I must have." Ego afflictions perpetuate the mental path of suffering that afflicts our thinking, well-being and anger. We all fall victim to ego afflictions at one time or another, and they are one of the root causes of our own suffering and anger and the suffering of others.

It is important to acknowledge that some parts of our ego are useful to survive. Without some ego or personality, the world would be a pretty bland place. Even great spiritual leaders possess a certain degree of ego in order to do their earthly work. The problem we have lies not in the positive traits of ego, but in the negative aspects of it.

Here's a quick review of the Five Patterns of Ego Affliction to help you understand any patterns you may have so you can begin to overcome them and move closer to uprooting your anger and suffering.

I am what I have. Let go of your need to have more, because *more* is never satisfied. Ironically, when you stop needing more, more of what you want will seem to arrive in your life. Materialism is counterproductive to happiness. People who value money and material possessions more than other life goals are less satisfied with their income and with their lives as a whole.

I am what I do. Let go of identifying yourself based on your achievements. We all come from the same place. When we lose the need to be superior, we begin to move toward a cooperative spirit with others.

I am what others think of me. Let go of your reputation, because it is not in *you* but in the minds of others. When we become attached to this reputation, there is often a tendency to live down to the expectations of others rather than soar beyond our limits.

I am separate from everyone. Let go of the belief that your suffering or accomplishments are unique. These beliefs distance you from others and increase isolation. It is also important to let go of the need to win and instead keep in mind that the opposite of winning is not always losing. Let go of the need to be right, because if you are always right, others must be wrong.

I am separate from God or a higher power. Let go of your illusion of separateness. Failure to find and tap into whatever floats your spiritual boat is failure to use a great source of energy that can propel you toward achievement. Stop being offended by people, their beliefs, and their situations in life.

That which offends you only weakens you.

The Three-Stage Process of Changing Thought

The path of omitting anger from your life begins with changing your thinking and is followed by both cognitive and behavioral change. The process of changing distorted and negative thinking, like that associated with anger, occurs in three stages.

1. The ability to identify and practice counterbalancing negative thoughts through concrete mental rehearsal

2. The conscious ability to actually counterbalance negative thoughts

3. The ability to subconsciously counterbalance negative thoughts

Stage One: Identifying and Counterbalancing Negative Thoughts

This first stage involves three steps:

1. Identify negative thoughts and patterns of negative thinking.

2. Write out the negative thoughts and then three counterbalancing and more positive thoughts. The most effective way is to make flashcards.

3. Rehearse your flashcards until the negative beliefs are reshaped and integrated into conscious thought.

First, you must concretely identify the distorted thinking behind your anger. To do this, you must pay attention to your overall thinking and specifically your patterns of distorted thought and the situations where you are most vulnerable. The goal is to create a list of the threads of your negative thoughts. It is essential to write these down to get them out of your head and into a concrete format.

It is important to identify and record the very center of your negative thinking and not engage in long journaling narratives of your suffering. I have seen many individuals who were counseled to journal their negative thinking in an effort to release the energy. My experience is that the exercise of journaling, while it can provide a cathartic release, serves as an exercise for emotional vomit and rehearsal of negative patterns of thinking. With practice comes improvement, and every time you rehearse your anger by writing and rereading your pain, you just get better at it. The same lesson applies to patterns of criticism, unrestrained fighting, and releasing your anger at inanimate objects.

The nature of most mental afflictions is to create patterns of negative thinking that ruminate in your head. People who have gone through episodes of clinical depression will tell you that, when isolating themselves, they are engaging in a pattern of negative thinking that becomes a negative feedback loop in their head. An important lesson can be learned by this pattern of negative thinking.

If you attempt to combat your negative thoughts by trying to counterbalance them in your head, you will lose the fight and often reinforce the negative patterns of thought.

You must identify and get the thoughts out of your head, rework them, and rehearse them back into your thinking. At the same time, it is helpful to identify the pattern of negative thinking to get a view of what your tendencies of distorted thought might be. For example:

I'm always getting the short end of the stick. (*Overgeneralization*)

My situation is all your fault. (*Blaming*)

I should have never listened to you. (*Should statement*)

I can tell they don't like me. (*Mind reading*)

To better understand the patterns that surround

your anger, it is also helpful to understand what situations and responses feed the pattern of angry thinking.

Personal Exercise: Log of Pain

In the table below, write what happened, what you struggled with, and your thoughts and pattern of thinking.

What happened?	What did you struggle with?	What were your thoughts and pattern of thinking?
Example: My friends didn't return my calls when I needed them.	Feeling abandoned in my time of need.	They should know I needed their support. See if I ever help them again. Should Statement/Personalization
1.		
2.		
3.		

4.		
5.		

In most cases, I find that people can easily identify a dozen negative thoughts when they do this exercise. These are often the core afflictive thoughts that contribute to anger and an overall lack of happiness.

The second part of this first stage of reshaping negative thoughts is to counterbalance your negative beliefs with three more positive thoughts that are based in reality. As part of this exercise, I recommend that you purchase a set of 5x7 spiral bound flash cards. The use of flash cards to actively rehearse your reframing of negative thoughts is an effective tool that is easy to use and can be retained. When setting up your cards, the "belief" can be taken from your log of pain.

The next challenge is to come up with three counterbalancing realities that effectively negate your negative beliefs. This is often a difficult challenge, because negative beliefs can be ingrained and an almost natural part of your thinking. Having someone like a friend, counselor or coach to help in this stage is beneficial. An outside party can offer an unattached perspective of the situation that is clear and unfettered. Here are some examples of how your flash cards should look:

Personal Exercise: Counterbalancing

Belief: They should know I need their support (should statement).

Reality: I must communicate my needs more directly.

I need to be more patient with my friends, because they also have busy lives.

I have a broad network of friends that I need to fully utilize.

Belief: People always treat me unfairly (overgeneralization).

Reality: Both friends and coworkers have treated me fairly.

I can learn to set better boundaries with others.

I need to focus more on the positive interactions I have with others.

Belief: If I don't do it perfectly, I have failed (all-or-nothing thinking).

Reality: Practice makes improvement, not perfection.

My pursuit of perfection is hurting me and negatively affecting others.

Few things in life are perfect, including me. I am only human.

Belief: They are such idiots. Can't they see that I am right? (being right)

Reality: The people I work with are competent.

Perhaps this is an opportunity for me to teach others.

My being right may not necessarily help the team.

Belief: I know this is going to turn out badly (catastrophizing).

Reality: I need to focus on the positive.

> I can ask for help if I need to.
>
> I have had success with this sort of thing in the past.

To advance to the second level of changing your thoughts, review these flash cards as much as possible until they become tattooed on your brain. The rate at which your thinking will change is directly connected to the amount of effort you put into reviewing these cards. I recommend that you place your note cards beside your bed and review them first thing in the morning and then again before going to sleep. Doing this seems to set the tone for the day and plant the seeds of change before sleep.

Stage Two: Consciously Counterbalance Negative Thoughts

With continued rehearsal of the flash cards you made in stage one, you will quickly notice yourself becoming more conscious of when negative thoughts and patterns begin to surface. Negative thoughts that once flew unnoticed by your conscious mind now rise to your surface of awareness where you can counterbalance them. As you do this, you are no longer bound to them as reality. At this stage, you can stop rehearsing your flashcards but, since patterns of negative thinking have the habit of resurfacing from time to time, keep them your cards where you can always have access to them.

Stage Three: Subconsciously Counterbalancing Negative Thoughts

If you have laid a good foundation for counterbalancing your negative thinking, the last stage of change is easy. Over time, you have concretely and consciously identified and challenged the negative thoughts that feed your anger. As you continue to challenge your negative thoughts, you will slowly find that the process becomes more subconscious than conscious. In other words, with enough repetition, your mind begins to identify negative thoughts and patterns of negative thoughts on its own and subconsciously negates them before they bubble to the surface of your awareness.

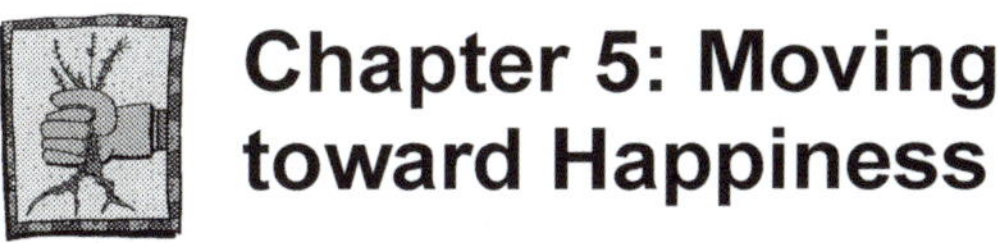 # Chapter 5: Moving toward Happiness

Happiness is a choice that requires effort at times.
—Aeschylus

When you are a teenager graduating from high school, the perception of having stress in your life is even greater than in adulthood. Most teenagers are eager to enter the larger world and long for the "freedom" that comes with going to college, getting a job, and living on their own. Yet, at this age, despite what we think at the time, we often lack the maturity and skills to manage what life's plan holds in store.

I was no different from most, in that I was confident, energetic and sometimes brash. I entered a small college in southern Minnesota and transferred after one year to the University of Minnesota. Stress does not respond well to the quick fixes or simple-minded solutions of youth. It is logical for us to want to avoid pain and escape stress, and we try many methods to accomplish this. Some people choose to manage their stress by walling themselves off and moving in a direction of isolation. Others attempt to anesthetize themselves somehow in an effort to escape life and further isolation. (If you were attending college in the late seventies, you might have anesthetized yourself just for the fun of it!) Many people, thankfully, do manage stress through healthy means of communication, physical activity or volunteerism.

I partied, studied and worked, but I began to experience increased feelings of anger that lay just below the surface of my everyday life. My anger began to seep into the nooks and crevices of friendships, relationships and concentration, and it began to feed that desire for escapism.

I knew that I didn't like my anger. I could see how it was affecting my performance and the people in my life. It became obvious to me that one major coping mechanism had been removed from my routine and that the resulting imbalance had to be part of my inability to manage my own anger. For the first time since my father walked me into a boxing gym at the age of eight, I was not playing a sport involving physical contact. In physical, competitive sports, the more you punish your opponent, and even yourself, the more you get to play and, hopefully, the more you win. This cycle can be a beautiful dance for an athlete. If you take it away, you must learn to adjust.

So my next logical step was to seek an activity that would help me replace the physical outlet I had lost. I enrolled in the kung fu club at the U of M and began my journey into martial arts and Eastern studies. The kung fu club was actually the largest club at the Twin Cities campus, which itself is one of the largest campuses in the country. The club met at the old field house in a large room with wooden walls and mats scattered in spots. I will always remember walking into the room and feeling massive in comparison to the other club members.

The U of M had a large Asian student population and I think all of them were members of the kung fu club. It was clear from the first day of class that there would be an emphasis on swift, flexible, circular movement, while I, in comparison, was rather bulky and linear in my movement.

When we first sparred, I felt very comfortable. My experience in boxing and familiarity with using my hands from football were assets. I moved well and jabbed at my opponent confidently when suddenly, Wham! My sparring partner did what I would later learn was an inside crescent kick right to the side of my head. The feeling was as humbling as being hit in the head with a frozen snowball thrown by a bully at fifty paces. I had never fought using feet, and it almost seemed unfair. I had much to learn; when practicing martial arts, school is always open.

Martial arts practice has continued to be a part of my life. As I made several moves around the country, a martial arts dojo was always a source of social interest, fitness training and education. Most importantly, I learned that having a physical outlet is a necessary tool for managing the physical energy that comes from anger. I have sometimes grown inconsistent in my training and, during these times, I notice how frustration, impatience and irritability begin to seep back into my daily life. Having an outlet for the physical effects of anger is an essential tool toward uprooting it. When you exercise, sweat, breathe, stretch, lift, walk, run and move, you cleanse your body of the toxic buildup resulting from stress and anger. Keep filling a tire with too much air and it will explode. Fail to release the energy associated with anger, in a healthy way, and you too will pop.

Researchers at Duke University Medical Center have also found that exercise can be a hefty weapon against depression. As reported in the *Archives of Internal Medicine* in 2000, 156 participants—all diagnosed with major depression—participated in a study on the effects of cardiovascular exercise on depression. In this study, the group attended three supervised classes a week in which they exercised on a treadmill or stationary bike at 70-85% of their maximum heart rate for thirty minutes. At the end of the four-month program, those who exercised reduced their rate of depression to the same degree as a group who took only antidepressants and another group who exercised *and* took antidepressants. Since irritability, depression and frustration are symptoms of anger, we can deduce that cardiovascular exercise is a necessary tool for your anger-prevention toolbox.

During my time studying at U of M, I continued to seek alternative ways to help me manage the destructive emotions I was experiencing. It was during this time that I bought my first motorcycle, began skydiving and took up road bicycling. Clearly, I developed an affinity for adrenaline, but underneath all this activity was a search for inner calm. There is a certain feeling of peace that comes on the tail of an adrenaline-charged activity. Like with an episode of anger, high adrenaline and exhaustive activities produce a decompressive calm after the storm. With these outlets now in place, my episodes of anger were greatly reduced. But I could tell this reduction was only the tip of the iceberg.

I studied journalism at the university, but eventually grew restless with the long, cold Minnesota winters. Although summers in Minnesota are wonderful, the seasons are limited for someone who enjoys pursuing two-wheeled activities on the road or launching themselves from an airplane. So I moved to Atlanta, rearranged my life, and reoriented my academics toward the field of psychology. It was through my study and work in the field of clinical psychology, along with continued studies in Eastern philosophy, that I further explored the intricacies of anger and destructive emotions.

Historically, the field of psychology has been consumed with a singular focus on mental illness. With almost an exclusive concentration on pathology, we have successfully developed quantifiable measures of conditions such as depression, anxiety, substance abuse, schizophrenia and personality disorders. There are theories to help us understand these disorders throughout a lifespan, and we have gained insight into the genetics, neurochemistry and psychological origins of mental illness. We have also developed pharmacological and therapeutic treatments for mental disorders that can greatly reduce the suffering experienced by those afflicted.

However, even as a young student of psychology, I always felt that something was missing. Why has this discipline been so focused on the negative? How did it venture onto a path where negative emotions are the norm and positive emotions are contrived or unoriginal?

I was never comfortable with calling individuals I worked with "patients" because this term always had a connotation of illness and somehow placed me above them. I always preferred to use the term "clients" because it is more indicative of a healthy modality and placed me on a more equal plane. The difference translated into an improved working relationship with my clients. If I could view them from a wellness perspective rather than an illness perspective, perhaps they could begin to also see themselves this way. What my clients quickly taught me is that they wanted more than to simply correct both their perceived and real weaknesses.

In over twenty years of clinical practice, I have been fortunate enough to work with the most chronic sufferers of mental illness. I have worked with adults who were both physically and mentally handicapped, addicts and soldiers of war. I have worked with people who have suffered horrific trauma and experienced the true evils of humankind. I have repeated conversations a hundred times over with older adults suffering from Alzheimer's disease. I have worked with corporate executives, athletes, actors and everyday heroes.

In every case, I have found a common theme that is often neglected in the field of psychology. People want lives that have meaning. They want more than to simply overcome their suffering and move on through life. In every case, with thousands of clients, I have learned that all people want one thing in their life: happiness. And so my focus as a clinician and coach has been shaped by this reality.

People want to reach far beyond developing their weaknesses. They strive for happiness that lasts longer than their suffering. People want to move beyond the doctrine of original sin or Sigmund Freud's theory of conflict and aggression.

The field of psychology is just beginning to fully research happiness. Positive psychology is a branch of psychological science that focuses on our individual pursuit of wellness and the good life, not just illness and overcoming it. In this context, I do not imply that the good life is found in material and financial gain, but I refer to the pursuit of the good life by using our strengths and having compassion for ourselves and others. However, the field of positive psychology has had to overcome some obstacles in its pursuit of understanding happiness.

At one time, psychologists believed that an individual's happiness had a set point, much like their weight, and so their happiness had a fixed range. Within this framework, people who were generally pessimistic or sad could not expect to achieve a great deal of happiness, and those whose style was happier were unlikely to become lastingly sad.

Another obstacle to the pursuit of studying happiness is the cynical belief that happiness is somehow fake or contrived. This belief cuts across many cultures and is rooted in the belief that we as humans are innately "rotten to the core" (Seligman, 2002). With such a pessimistic view of our human nature, it is no wonder that anger plagues our lives.

Contrary to this belief is the Buddhist perspective that the very purpose of our life is to seek happiness. In his book, *The Art of Happiness*, His Holiness the Dalai Lama states that "the very motion of our life is toward happiness." From this perspective, the Dalai Lama believes that happiness can be achieved by training the mind and transforming the heart and spirit through discipline and a transformation of attitude. Therefore, the challenge is how to cultivate greater happiness and extinguish the destructive emotions that undermine this pursuit.

What Is Our Nature?

Cumulative scientific research indicates that aggression and violent behavior in man is not innate. Instead, they are shaped more by outside factors, including biological, social, environmental, and situational influences. It is scientifically incorrect to say that we have a predisposition toward aggression and violence. Even though we have the capacity to make war, aggression is not an automatic response.

Contrary to the belief that we are inherently aggressive is supporting research indicating that humans have a naturally prosocial disposition and a tendency toward altruistic behavior (Batson, Shaw, 1991). In fact, humans have an instinctive tendency to develop close bonds with one another and to work for the betterment of others as well as for ourselves. As a matter of fact, this tendency toward social interest and our need to work together is more likely to be the foundation of our survival instinct than our capacity for aggression. I believe that our nature is innately compassionate and that, although we get angry, that anger arises at a lesser level than is our true nature.

Benefits of Happiness

There are many benefits to cultivating happiness in our life and in the lives of others. Optimistic people tend to interpret life's challenges as a passing moment that is controllable. In contrast, pessimists often believe that their troubles will always exist and are uncontrollable. Happy people are inclined to endure pain better and their positive emotions tend to counterbalance negative emotions. Happy people seem to forget bad events more readily and remember more good events than might have actually happened. Happy people tend to be more productive and miss work less often. Happy people spend less time alone and more time in social settings because, when we're happy, we like other people more and want to share our happiness. When we are down, we become selfish, defensive and closed off.

Roadblocks to Happiness

In assessing the roadblocks to achieving happiness, we must first acknowledge the predispositions that influence our individual makeup. We are each likely to have our own set point, or range, for happiness. When positive events happen in our life, we are likely to return to our baseline level of happiness. Consequently, we will be pulled up toward this baseline after experiencing an unhappy or negative life event. Therefore, a low set point for happiness is likely to be a roadblock, while a high set point is likely to be an asset to overall happiness.

Predispositions are also linked to a person's temperament and degree of optimism or pessimism. While predispositions may be a roadblock, our temperament is malleable and subject to change. The human mind and body are adaptive, flexible and re-generative.

As discussed earlier, modernization and the environment it produces cause a variety of stress and ills. We are more sedentary, eat large quantities of fat on the go, and overindulge in processed sugars. We pollute the environment, sit in traffic, breath bad air, and frequently calm ourselves with alcohol, drugs, cigarettes or prescription medications. The effects of modernization and our capacity to adapt to rapid change is a direct barrier to cultivating happiness.

Our incredible ability to adapt also raises another barrier to achieving greater happiness. Seligman, in his book, *Authentic Happiness,* calls our ability to adapt to good things in life the "hedonic treadmill." The hedonic treadmill refers to our ability to adapt and become bored with positive change. Seligman points out the ease with which we can take things for granted and how our expectations begin to rise with the accumulation of possessions and accomplishments. On the opposite end are negative life occurrences that we may never adapt to, such as the loss of a loved one or prolonged circumstances of suffering.

Negativity corrodes the human spirit and is a pervasive barrier to achieving happiness. A negative attitude is self-defeating and perpetuates nothing more than a negative outcome. Pervasive negative thinking invites negative behavior, distances us from other people, and reinforces a downward spiral of complaints and damaging outcomes. Where our mind wanders, so will follow our behavior and emotions. With enough work, patterns of negative thinking can become a loop of self-hypnosis that programs us for failure.

So, if inherent traits, modernization, the hedonic treadmill and negativity serve as barriers to happiness, what directly influences happiness?

Happiness and Social Interest
The old saying is that misery loves company but, based on recent research, it is happiness, not misery, that does. A new study by researchers at Harvard University and the University of California, San Diego (UCSD) reveals how happiness spreads through social networks.

According to a recent article published by the *British Medical Journal,* the Farmingham Heart Study also researched the spread of emotion through social connections and found that happiness spreads readily through social networks of family members, friends and neighbors. According to Nicholas Christakis, a professor at Harvard Medical School and coauthor of the study, "Everyday interactions we have with other people are definitely contagious, in terms of happiness." He also says, "Your emotional state depends not just on actions and choices that you make, but also on actions and choices of other people, many of which you don't even know."

Christakis and coauthor James H. Fowler, of UCSD, discovered that happy people in geographic proximity are most effective in spreading their good cheer. They also found that the happiest people are often found at the center of large social networks. In other words, happiness tends to spread like a positive virus.

Visualize a party and the social dynamics. You are likely to see people who are on the fringes or talking one-on-one in the corners. You will also have people in the center of the room having conversations with many people. According to the research by Christakis and Fowler, those in the center of the room will be among the happiest. "We think the reason is because those in the center of the room are more susceptible to the waves of happiness that spread throughout the network," explains Fowler.

The Farmingham Heart Study reveals that being with someone who is happy makes you 15.3 % more likely to be happy yourself. A happy friend whom you see often increases your odds of happiness by 9.8%, and even your neighbor's sister's friend can give you a 5.6% boost in overall happiness by being happy. Similarly, happy siblings can make you 14% more likely to be happy yourself, but only if you see them regularly. Happy spouses provide an 8% boost in happiness if they live under the same roof, and joyful next-door neighbors make you 34% more likely to be happy when associating with them.

While proximity and geographic location are important variables to happiness, Christakis and

Fowler suspect that friends or family whom you don't see on a regular basis contribute less to your happiness. There is no substitute for face-to-face interaction; getting connected by phone or the Internet is not the same.

What Influences Happiness?

In an effort to generate more happiness and less anger in your life, let's look at those factors known to influence happiness and those that don't:

State of Mind. It is true that happiness is more greatly influenced by our state of mind than by the external events in our life. Happiness most often depends on how we perceive our situation and how satisfied we are with life.

Genetics. Although our genetics influence our set point for happiness, there is evidence to support our ability to enhance this range and elevate our baseline of happiness.

Democracy. Living in a wealthy democracy has a strong influence on happiness when compared to living in an impoverished dictatorial society.

Marriage. Marriage and stable relationships have a strong influence on happiness.

Inner Contentment. You can go about obtaining everything you could possibly desire and eventually run into something you can't have, or you can learn to want and appreciate what you already have.

Social Interest. The development of a social network and an enhanced sense of contribution to others produce a robust effect on happiness.

Self-Comparison. When you consistently compare yourself to others, you will most often end up focusing on your own shortcomings. When you're caught in the ego affliction of "I am what others think of me," you will most likely live down to their expectations.

Inner Worth. Like many things, inner worth is not cultivated in isolation. Instead, it comes from the realization that we are part of the human community. Remembering this bond is important to cultivating a sense of inner worth and dignity.

Healthy Aging. Good health has a tremendous influence on our happiness. In George E. Vaillant's "Grant Study," which studied the human life cycle of men over the course of thirty years, verified that smoking, alcohol use and unhealthy weight contribute greatly to unhealthy aging.

An Adaptive Coping Style*.* Simply put, the ability to adapt to your environment and develop coping skills to manage an ever-changing world is a key factor in both happiness and overall well-being.

Religion and Spirituality. People who believe in religion or spirituality are less likely to experience substance abuse, get divorced, commit crimes or kill themselves. Surveys consistently show that religious and spiritual people are, to a moderate degree, happier than nonreligious or nonspiritual people.

Cultivating Gratitude

I often talk with clients about the importance of "cultivating" happiness. Sometimes the ground is soft and joy comes bubbling through with ease. Then there are other times in life when the ground is as hard as Georgia clay in a draught and we need a jackhammer to cultivate the tiniest glimmer of happiness. If we are lucky, life will present us with an abundance of happiness, but many times, we must work at it and understand that happiness is cultivated by effort and what we give to others.

It is true that regularly counting your blessings can increase your overall happiness and contentment with life. As a society, Americans have few rituals for expressing our gratitude to others who have been helpful. Think of all the people who have helped you in your life and how often you have made a specific effort to thank them. The truth is that direct expressions of gratitude have a strong correlation to overall happiness.

I often ask clients to write a letter of gratitude for this very reason. Additionally, I ask them to deliver the letter and, if possible, have the person read the letter back to them. I have had clients write letters to their parents, friends, siblings, coaches, bosses and teachers. Here are some guidelines for writing a letter of gratitude:

Personal Exercise: Letter of Gratitude

Think of someone who truly helped you or made a positive impact on your life.

Write a letter of gratitude that describes in concrete terms when and how they helped you.

Describe how this help influenced your life at that time and going forward.

Describe how you hope their counsel will serve to guide you in the future.

Express heartfelt thanks for their kindness and your well wishes for the future.

Letters of gratitude are one of the few exercises I recommend that produce 100% positive return on investment. You will feel grateful and your recipient will as well.

Another technique for cultivating gratitude and happiness is the technique of writing down three things that went well and/or that you are grateful for each day (Seligman, Steen, Park and Peterson, 2005). I generally recommend that you do this at the end of each day in a journal or notebook that you can keep beside the bed.

This exercise is simple, but has a strong impact on positive thinking and happiness. The commitment of writing three positive things each day shapes the mindset of looking for positive events throughout the day. With this outlook, there is a mental shift toward the positive. Even on dreary days, where everything seems to go wrong, this practice forces you to turn over even the smallest rock to find a positive. An additional reinforcement of this strategy is to share your grateful events with someone else. My wife, daughter and I do this each evening, much like a prayer, and it not only cultivates, but also spreads, a feeling of happiness.

Personal Exercise: Being Grateful
Write three things that you are grateful for today. Do this at the end of every day and be attentive to how this exercise elevates your overall happiness:

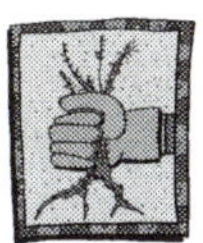# Chapter 6: Finding Your North Star

In the absence of clearly defined goals, we become strangely loyal to performing daily trivia until ultimately we become enslaved by it.   —Robert Heinlein

The importance of setting goals became very clear to me as I studied and began work in the field of psychology. The long-term goal of advanced education, coupled with working my way through school and continuing to practice martial arts, mandated that I set both short-term, mid-range and long-term goals. It was during this time that I learned the value of self-evaluation. It was important that I identify my own vulnerabilities and how they were likely to affect my ability to reach the goals I was setting.

For example, I had to learn and acknowledge that I had a tendency to start fast, do well, and then lose momentum in the middle of the semester so I would have to really cram at the end to save my grade. I had a tendency to put papers off and do my best work under the gun, so I often turned in assignments while the ink was still wet. I also learned that I would make commitments to others that I really didn't have time to fulfill, like researching projects and attending study groups. I would always keep my commitment, but I was trying to accomplish too much.

Goal-Oriented Movement and Resilience

You learn a lot about setting goals from being involved in both team and individual competitive sports. There are long-term goals of having a successful season or personal goals of post-season recognition. There are mid-range goals that focus on winning a specific match and how you are going to best position yourself for victory. Then there are more short-term goals of how you and/or your team are going to specifically execute against an opponent and beat them.

Setting goals is also a necessary part of getting a successful education. While most people set the long-term goal of completing college, many students change majors several times as they readjust what they want to focus on. It often seems that the farther out we set our goals, the more uncertain they become. There are the goals of completing each undergraduate year, applying to the school of our major, and scrounging enough money to pay for books. Then there are the short-term goals of passing each class, conducting research for a paper, and getting to that early-morning economics class when the temperature outside is sinking below zero.

Those who create success in life most often do so by setting goals of varied ranges and pursuing them until completion. The path toward goal completion is as varied and unique as the individuals who set them. Some athletes spend hours in the weight room and study film of their opponents until their eyes pop out. Others practice and play, relying only on the gifts God gave them. Some students graduate from college in four years; others take twice as long. No matter how you go about achieving your goals, the key is to set them and remain diligent enough to eventually achieve them.

For all of us there comes a point in life when we must learn to focus and refine our thoughts regarding what kind of person we want to be and what kind of life we want to live. By its very definition, life is about movement, and we are constantly faced with the challenge of choosing which path to move along. Fight or flight, move forward or withdraw—these choices in life define how it will play out. We all make good and bad choices, and most of us learn to live with the consequences of each.

We all start out like a seedling, vulnerable to nature and dependent. As we begin to grow, it is our choices in the battle against life's elements that build strength. If we are fortunate, we face enough storms and life changes to help us grow rooted and strong. Like a tree, we grow some bark that provides us with the protection and resilience to withstand the challenges of life and nature. Anger is a short-term solution and an ill-suited coping style for the long struggle of a lifespan.

Psychological and physical resilience is the positive capacity of people to cope with stress and catastrophe.

Although I would roll my eyes every time my father spoke about how his generation suffered through "the great depression" and "WWII," he was right about one thing: Those experiences tested his generation's metal, and the result was greater resilience in their ability to manage life's suffering.

Resilience is directly related to a person's ability to cope with future negative events with an accumulation of "protective factors" in life. Resilience is often measured against the cumulative "risk factors" we face or take in life. While I would say that my pursuit of risk-taking behaviors, like riding motorcycles, practicing martial arts and skydiving have positively affected my psychological resilience, they have also taken a toll on my physical resilience.

Some people go through life well protected from life's challenges; they are less likely to develop their resilience to negative life events. On the other hand, there are people who are overly exposed to life's hardships and may find their resilience broken down over time. As it is with most things, we hope to find a balance of life experiences and exposure to risk that strengthens us but doesn't break down the protective benefits of resilience.

Alfred Adler, founder of individual psychology, believed that an individual's movement through life is goal-directed or teleological in nature, and that our behavior is generally purposeful. This teleological point of view sees life as moving ahead, futuristically oriented and goal-determined. People are mostly practical in life, and we tend to stick with whatever coping styles we've developed and perceive as working. When our behaviors no longer work and a change in coping style is necessary, we begin to struggle. I find that most people, whether consciously or unconsciously, stated or not stated, do move toward some goal in life.

H.H. the Dalai Lama would say that we are all moving toward the goal of "happiness" and I too believe this. Alfred Adler would point out that man does not build life alone. Instead, man builds on the shoulders of others who have gone before and also builds for those who will come after. In terms of social interest, man ideally progresses hand in hand with others toward the goal of a better—or even perfect—world.

I don't believe we are deterministically pushed through life by our environment, causes and events. Instead, I agree with Adler's belief that we are pulled through life by our own dynamic strivings and goals. The belief that we are victims of our causes or events has always been somewhat speculative to me. Individuals react differently to similar situations because we all have certain perspectives that color our life experiences.

Humans also have free will, which we use daily in the decisions we make. Even though causal events from our past can't be changed, our goals, once they are recognized, offer a choice. We can choose to continue as we did before (but no longer in innocence, which makes the old behavior less palatable) or we can make a change that is usually more encouraging and provides a goal to shoot for. I have found this goal-oriented approach toward personal change to be an effective and empowering model that generates movement.

Setting goals and defining what matters to you are essential steps to any course correction in life, such as choosing to uproot your anger. Ultimately, you must define a direction for your life change. Now is the time to take a bold step toward the direction you want for change and identify specific targets for change.

This target must become a North Star that serves as your axis point for thought and behavior. A well-defined goal serves as a polar-star navigational point for guiding your decisions and keeping a steady course, and as a measure for course correction so you can make changes before being blown too far from the heavens.

Too often people are caught up in a pattern of fishtailing through life. They swim back and forth, constantly drifting off course. These patterns often result in the need for frequent and sweeping course corrections that drain time and energy. I have seen people set sail in life without a map or destination, and others who have both a map and destination point but never take the time to refer to their planned course. Goals that serve as our North Star don't vary and, while the winds of change will inevitably blow us off course, the correction is not as great if you keep your eye on that singular point of light.

Think of when you first had the goal of learning to ride a bicycle and you wobbled the front wheel back and forth in huge gyrations while keeping balance. After some practice, and a few falls, you learned to ride the bike by making course corrections that were so smooth and subtle that your path was straight, balanced and controllable. Establishing goals is like setting your sights on a target that guides your conduct each day and advances your progress and improvement until your course corrections become almost unnoticed.

Healthy Balance and Targets for Change

Short-term goals are points that are attainable in the near future; long-term goals are farther down the road. Establishing both short-term and long-term goals makes for an evenly paced journey that leads from one step to the next. Short-term goals frequently fall into the range of maintaining a healthy life balance, which requires frequent identification and behavioral adjustment. Success with these short-term objectives lays the foundation for long-term goal achievement. Healthy life balance frequently involves these five areas:

1. Physical balance

2. Mental balance

3. Emotional balance

4. Social balance

5. Spiritual balance

In our superheated society, we are in a constant battle to take care of ourselves, our family, our children, our home and our career while maintaining our physical health, soul, mental stability, friendships and compassionate volunteerism. Unfortunately, there are no easy formulas for committing yourself to these relationships and responsibilities while remaining responsive to your own ever-changing emotions and needs. The dilemma of maintaining a healthy balance is a tightrope walk of investing yourself in self-care, care of others, a meaningful life, and work you can be proud of.

Everyone determines which aspects of their healthy balance are most important to them. We prioritize the best we can and target some aspects of health to give special attention to. Sometimes I really need to focus on getting in my workouts and watching what I eat. Next month I may notice that my spiritual efforts have fallen short and I will invest greater energy in this. Achieving and maintaining a healthy life balance is a constant fluctuation in identification, prioritization and effort. Because we have a tendency to ignore our own needs, it helps to have a tool to help evaluate our current balance.

Personal Exercise: Healthy Balance Assessment

I have used the following Healthy Balance worksheet, adapted from *Seeking Your Healthy Balance* by Tubesing and Tubesing, for years. When done often enough, this assessment can help you adjust to your changing needs, maintain course, and not deviate from your North Star. I recommend that you ask yourself these questions at least once a month, because change happens fast!

Comment on your current level of balance in the following areas. Be specific and use examples when you can.

Physical Health:
I'm____

Mental Health:
I'm____

Emotional Health:
I'm____

Social Health:
I'm____

Spiritual Health:
I'm____

Complete this sentence: I feel most alive when:

____
____

Aspects of my health I would like to improve:

____
____

Complete the following statement: If I want my health to improve, I need to stop

____
____

And I need to start

____
____

This worksheet helps identify where your equilibrium is discordant and where you need to make adjustments to maintain a healthy life balance. The sentence "I feel most alive when" is a useful and revealing diagnostic question I have used effectively with clients for years. If I feel most alive when hiking in the woods, sailing on the water, motorcycling or playing with my daughter, and if I am feeling somewhat out of balance, I know that I probably have not invested enough time in these activities recently. Individuals suffering significant life stress or illness will easily identify a pattern of movement away from what makes them "feel alive." The solution is always obvious, and the line of movement is always toward something enjoyable.

After identifying the area(s) where you are out of balance, brainstorm some remedies of what you can do to create movement toward greater balance. Again, it is always best to write these opportunities down and post them in a conspicuous place. (As always, there is greater benefit to including a social line of movement to these remedies, such as walking with a friend, joining a book club, taking a gardening class, etc.) I call this "refrigerator material" for reminding me of the direction I want to be moving. So write your remedies and place them on your refrigerator as a reminder to move in the right direction.

Personal Exercise: Healthy Balance Remedies

Brainstorm some of the health remedies you use for improving your healthy balance.

Physical	Mental/ Emotional	Social	Spiritual
Walk	Read	Laugh	Pray/meditate
______	______	______	______
______	______	______	______
______	______	______	______
______	______	______	______
______	______	______	______
______	______	______	______
______	______	______	______
______	______	______	______
______	______	______	______
______	______	______	______
______	______	______	______
______	______	______	______

Clarifying Your Values and Moral Compass

Personal values are a belief, a mission or a philosophy that is personally meaningful. They serve as the guideposts for making decisions about right and wrong, good and bad, should I? and shouldn't I? Most personal values have their foundation in our past and can have their origin in the family and community values we grew up with. In addition, we are exposed to countless other values and life events that shape our value system. These value systems are flexible and often change throughout a lifespan. Values can range from the commonplace, such as a belief in hard work and punctuality, to the more psychological, such as self-reliance, compassion and harmony of purpose. Whether we are consciously aware of our values or not, every individual has a core set.

If we are going to explore what values are, we

must understand what values are *not*. Values go beyond words and into the realm of our thoughts and behaviors. If we are not careful, values can become distorted by patterns of negative thinking and become counterproductive. Values differ from goals in that goals are concrete and achievable events, situations or objects. Goals can be changed, possessed and completed, while values are more enduring and less tangible.

Values are not feelings, but there are frequently feelings that accompany our choices in life. Although you can live your life according to your values, which often leads to success, values are *directions* in life, not *outcomes*. Adherence to our values doesn't mean that our path is always going to be straight. You will inevitably face obstacles that will force you to change direction. Also, we are human and, as such, we will sometimes zig when we meant to zag.

Clarifying your personal values is an essential part of learning to move beyond your anger. They will serve as guidelines for your decision-making and streamline the path toward all your goals. If every life decision you make remains congruent with your personal values, you are likely to end up where you want to be. If your goal is to uproot your anger and you have a personal value of being kind or compassionate to other people, the chances of becoming less angry are much higher.

Personal Exercise: Personal Values
Use this list as a guideline to identify your top values. Initially, circle ten values that are most important to your behavior. Add any values of your own to this list.

Accountability	Financially	Physical
Achievement	secure	challenge
Adventure-	Freedom	Pleasure
some	Friendly	Power
Affectionate	Growth-oriented	Privacy
Artistic	Helpful	Public service
Challenge	Honest	Quality
Change	Independent	Recognition
Close relation-	Influential	Religion
ships	Integrity	Reputation
Community	Intellectual	Respect
Compassion	Involved	Responsibility
Confident	Knowledgeable	Security
Cooperative	Leader	Self-respect
Creative	Living fast	Serenity
Decisive	Loyal	Sophistication
Democratic	Marketable	Stability
Direct	Meaningful	Status
Economical	Merit	Supervising
Effective	Money	others
Efficient	Nature	Time
Environmental	Order	Truth
Ethical	Personal	Wealth
Excited	Personable	Wisdom
Faith		

Now narrow these values down to your top five and record them below. Next to each value, record where that value has come from in your life (father, mother, family, community, own experience, etc.). Finally, rate how you are currently doing with each value on a scale of 1-10, with 10 being the highest. If your value is honesty and you are always a 100% honest, give yourself a 10.

Value	Origin of this value	How you're doing on this value (1-10)
1.		
2.		
3.		
4.		
5.		

Now you have a refined list of your top values as a guideline for your goals and decision-making. The origin of each value adds weight to its importance. Any value scores of six and below are opportunities for improvement and/or additional goal setting. In most cases, your values will be incongruent with anything related to anger, as it would be rare for someone to have a value of hurting themselves or other people.

Goal Setting

As the old saying goes, "If you can dream it, you can achieve it." But too often, we find ourselves simply dreaming and wondering why life has left us short, as our dreams become distant memories. Even worse is when our unrealized dreams become a source of negative belief or resentment toward the world and our place in it.

The biggest failure with unrealized dreams lies in our inability to establish goals. If our values are guiderails toward reaching our result, then goals can lead us there. Goals are the mile markers that guide and measure your journey through life and what you want to achieve. They allow you to manifest your values in the world. Goals achieved serve as positive reinforcement for continued movement. Goals we struggle with, or fail to achieve, are opportunities for reevaluating or overcoming.

There are generally three paths people take when approaching their goals. These paths are a reflection of the important concept of courage. Courage is what helps us use our inner resources and is the embodiment of self-confidence. It is our willingness to take a chance and stems from our faith in our own ability. Courage is developed by daring to take a risk and meet a challenge. A lack of courage is more likely to lead us down the more useless side of life. It takes courage to admit our imperfections and courage to be humble. It takes more courage to restrain your anger than it does to unleash it on others, and anger absolutely moves us toward the useless side of life.

The three paths of approaching goals reflect three levels of courage, and I look at this from the perspective of climbing a mountain:

High Courage. These individuals set their sights on the mountain summit (goal) and they climb vigorously with a single-minded purpose of reaching the peak. This approach is generally efficient, challenging, higher risk and headed toward the more useful side of life. The climber has hopefully trained and, while climbing, he primarily sees an immediate and peripheral view of the mountain surface. While this approach can be a group effort, it is often a solo approach and it's difficult to add supportive members in midclimb. A team that works efficiently together throughout the climb can add to the reward, but stragglers can be a source of irritability and impatience. People who approach their goals in this way generally move with purpose and experience great exhilaration when they reach the summit.

Moderate Courage. These individuals choose to tackle the mountain by traversing a path up a more manageable grade. With this approach, they see more of the mountain as they patiently move upward and negotiate a variety of grades and terrains. This approach often follows paths where others have walked before and presents a more moderate risk. Movement is most often on the useful side of life. This approach allows more time to adjust the degree of challenge and provides more opportunities for rest and evaluation. People who choose this approach are more likely to be joined by others who provide both social support and the challenge of typical group dynamics. Like the first group, this approach moves with purpose, but the climbers take more time to smell the roses. They also experience great exhilaration when the summit is reached.

Low Courage. These individuals prefer to walk around the base of the mountain on familiar ground. They look up at the beauty of the mountain and see a great deal of it, but from a distance. This approach is low risk and may lead down the useless path of life. These individuals may gain great knowledge of the mountain, but will lack the experiential learning from being challenged by the mountain itself. This approach may be solo or may involve high social interest. It is a low-risk approach that lacks the exhilaration of the previous two styles. People who circle the mountain may be content, but they often struggle for the courage to challenge life. They may set the bar lower, yet long for accomplishment and therefore feel unfulfilled.

The second-level climbers' approach is best suited to the goal of overcoming issues of anger. Uprooting anger requires the patience developed by an enduring climb. It requires a good vantage point from which to see what is coming. Uprooting anger requires high social interest and a broad awareness of the environment and ourselves. It requires courage and a commitment to move toward the useful side of life.

In developing your goals, you will need to consider both short-term and long-term objectives. As we've discussed, short-term goals are stops we can get to in the near future. Long-term goals take more time. Establishing both short-term and long-term goals make for a well-paced and comprehensive climb up the mountain. Although we can meander around the mountain until we find the top, a goal-oriented climb is more practical and efficient.

Successful goal setting involves several short-term goals that build toward the eventual long-term objective. There are six steps to assuring successful goal setting.

1. Set goals that are congruent and in line with your personal values. There is no chance of success otherwise.

2. Make sure your goals are something you want, not goals someone else wants or that just sound good.

3. Develop goals that address the five areas of healthy balance: physical, mental, emotional, social and spiritual well-being.

4. Write positive goals that reflect what you *want*, not what you want to leave behind.

5. Write goals that are not dependent on the actions of others. The goal of wanting to change some-

one else's emotions or actions is nice, but it is dependent on them, not you.

6. Set **SMART** goals:

S = Specific

M= Measurable

A = Attainable

R = Realistic

T = Timely

Specific

Goals should be straightforward and focused on what you want to happen. Specifically defining what you are going to do helps focus your efforts.

Setting specific goals means answering the what, why and how of your objective.

What are you going to do? Use action words not theory.

Why is this goal important at this time and how does it relate to the overall goal of what you want to accomplish?

How are you going to do it?

Make the answers to the above questions specific, clear and easy. Instead of saying that you will eliminate your anger, set goals of exercising four days a week and not unleashing your anger on anyone.

Measurable: If you can't measure your progress, you are not likely to be able to manage it. Write a goal for which you can measure progress and know when you have reached your target. Set observable dates, limits and expectations for your behavior.

Attainable: Goals must be attainable and stretch your abilities slightly so that you feel you can do it. Goals that are too out of reach may be defeating and you run the risk of losing your commitment. Success creates more motivation.

Realistic: Realistic in this case means setting goals that are "doable," ensuring that you have the skills needed to do the work. Set the bar high enough and devise a strategy or a way of getting there that makes the goal realistic.

Timely: Set a time frame for your goals: next week; three months; three, five and ten years. Putting an ending point on your goal gives you a clear target to work toward.

Set times and dates for completion so your commitment isn't too vague. Goals frequently get stuck on the launching pad when you feel that you can start at any time. Create a sense of urgency to take action now.

Personal Exercise: Goal-Setting Worksheet

Today's Date: _______________________________

Which value does this goal apply to?

____

Which area of healthy balance does this goal apply to?
Physical   Mental   Emotional   Social   Spiritual

____

Long-Term Goal:

____
____
____

Short-Term Goal:

____
____
____

Verify that your goal is SMART:

Specific: *What exactly will you accomplish?*

____

____

____

Measurable: *How will you know when you have reached this goal?*

____

____

____

Achievable: *Is achieving this goal within your abilities and commitment? Do you have the resources to achieve this goal? If not, how will you get them?*

____

____

____

Relevant: *Why is this goal significant to your life?*

____

____

____

Timely: *When will this goal be achieved?*

____

____

____

Defining Barriers

Inevitably, there will be challenges that threaten your progress toward even the most defined goals. Some barriers involve practical solutions, while others are more complicated. If your goal is to overcome your anger, barriers will likely emerge in the form of old demons of thought or past events that you've tried to avoid.

We often feel blindsided by these barriers, but

the reality is that we often just fail to see them coming. Therefore, when setting goals, try to anticipate what barriers you might face and brainstorm a strategy for overcoming them.

Personal Exercise: Barrier Identification

Use the table below to help define barriers to your goals and brainstorm strategies to overcome them. What barriers or challenges can you anticipate and what is your strategy for overcoming them?

Anticipated Barriers	Strategies to Overcome
1.	
2.	
3.	
4.	
5.	

Statement of Intent

So far, we have discussed the dynamics of goal setting in broad terms, but you knew before opening this book that your long-term goal is to overcome or uproot the toxic anger in your life. While setting goals for changing thoughts and behaviors is an effective approach to change, public statements of our intentions can be a driving force for commitment and consistent change. Therefore, I often challenge clients to form their values, long-term goals and short-term goals into what I call a statement of intent. So let's look at some of my long- and short-term goals regarding anger and sprinkle them with some of my own values to form a statement of intent. Of course, you can use these if they fit, but it would be better to form your own statement of intent relating to your own goals and values.

Long-Term Goals for Anger:

I will never again unleash my anger on others.

I will work each day toward uprooting my anger.

Top Personal Values:

Compassion

Honesty

Family

Short-Term Goals:

I will work out vigorously four times a week.

I will take a time-out and remove myself from a situation before responding in anger.

I will practice meditation four days a week for at least thirty minutes.

Statement of Intent: *Each day, I will treat others with honesty and selfless compassion. I will not unleash my anger on anyone and will find peace through regular exercise and meditation.*

I will treat the world as my family and remove myself from any situation where my anger might arise.

This statement of intent has become my mission and I share it with others. I have written it out and placed it in conspicuous places like my bathroom mirror and my office. I incorporated this statement as a mantra in my meditation and rehearse it as prayer when I struggle. Over time, it has become both a conscious and unconscious guide for my behavior. I've learned to keep these reminders conspicuous because the winds of change can take me off course. There are also times when I can become complacent and need a visible reminder to help me regain my course (refrigerator material). This statement of intent is my North Star that guides me toward the goal of uprooting anger.

Now it's time for you to establish write your statement of intent. Review your long-term goal of omitting anger, your values, and your short-term objectives. Craft your statement of intent and place it in a visible place so it can serve as constant reminder of the direction you are moving. Writing your statement on index cards and putting them on the bathroom mirror, refrigerator and/or desk is a simple and effective strategy.

Exercise: Statement of Intent

____

____

____

____

____

____

____

____

____

Chapter 7: Expanding Your Toolbox

We shall not fail or falter; we shall not weaken or tire. Give us the tools and we will finish the job.
—Sir Winston Churchill

Relationships are hard work and, if anger is ever going to reveal itself, it will be with our partners and those closest to us. My wife has been a part of my journey in overcoming my issues of anger and, although she has her battle scars, she has been fully adept at dishing out her own brand of Southside Chicago justice. We like to think that our arguments and issues of anger have added "spice" to our relationship, and there is no question that these struggles have made us more resilient and stronger as a couple. The journey of working toward the omission of anger has been a mutual effort, not just mine, so it is important in relationships to understand that it usually does take two to tangle and two to heal.

I have worked with couple-clients who were under the impression that only the person with anger is in need of change. The task of overcoming anger within a relationship is much harder if one partner continues to bring up past issues of harm or resentments, and change is nearly impossible if patterns of criticism continue in the relationship.

Relationships

Patterns of anger and argument in relationships become an unhealthy dance. A challenge usually rises when one person makes a decision to change the dance steps. When working on uprooting anger, partners must adjust and learn to follow these new dance steps to make a relational change. Without this adjustment, partners are likely to end up with two separate and incongruent dances going on in the relationship. Out of sync and short on style points.

As a counselor and coach, I am amazed at the dynamics of anger in relationships, but there are familiar patterns we can learn from. For example, it is true that those we love most usually get the worst of our anger; perhaps this is due to our comfort and proximity.

I also know that it is the dynamic of most emotional disorders to move us in the direction of isolation, and that anger, as a symptom of these disorders, serves to push others away. If our anger can distance us from those who are closest to us, we truly become isolated and alone. Research in the field of marital counseling can help us better understand struggles within relationships.

Most of the things that couples are fighting about today will be the same things they will fight about a decade from now. According to John Gottman, PhD, professor of family psychology at the University of Washington in Seattle, couples argue about the same issues 69% of the time. His long-term studies of more than 670 couples show that couples rarely resolve these issues because many of the problems are actually unsolvable.

Couples who remarry, or change partners, seemingly inherit sets of new and unresolved issues. "It's a myth that if you solve your problems you'll automatically be happy," says Gottman. "We need to teach couples that they'll never solve most of their problems." He contends that the way to happiness is to "establish a dialogue" around the problems and learn to live and adapt to them in much the same way someone learns to live with a bad back or physical limitation.

The challenge is to acknowledge your partner's

limitations, encourage improvement and still communicate acceptance of them as a person and a partner. This is something we often do in our friendships but struggle to do in marriage.

Marriage and money are scarcely a civil union. Couples fight about money more than any other issue, and this is as true of couples who remain married as of couples who wind up divorcing. The main financial matters couples fight over include:

• Debts (credit card and other).

• Levels of spending and saving. (Women tend to think men should make more, men tend to think women should spend less.)

• Time spent working.

• Differences in long-term financial goals (such as retirement savings).

• Money chores (such as balancing the checkbook and paying bills).

Sometimes it seems as if couples fight over nothing, but there are frequently patterns to the arguments, often unconscious. Several things precipitate these unwanted arguments, such as resentment, habit, emotional states and even boredom.

In some cases, arguments and their patterns are precipitated by poor communication or how things are phrased. Poorly-phrased communication can lead to misunderstandings and arguments. While we will be discussing communication in more depth in Chapter 8, we will briefly touch on some roadblocks to relational communication. In many cases, couples slip into patterns of criticism that can be the death knell of a relationship. Patterns of criticism are the quickest way to undermine a relationship and feed anger.

I often encourage couples to focus on framing things as a complaint instead of a criticism, but the more engrained the pattern, the harder it is to turn around. A complaint is very specific while criticism is very broad in content. For example, a complaint would be "It would have helped me if you had prepared dinner tonight." The criticism would be "You never help out when I need it."

Communication is a two-way street that involves speaking and listening. The challenge with changing patterns of criticism lies not only in the spoken message but in how the receiver is hearing the message. In other words, you can make progress in eliminating patterns of criticism, but very often, our partners will continue to hear criticism even when it is not there, simply because the pitch, tone or message has become ingrained in the couple's communication.

The way we communicate can also become a game of word ping-pong devoid of listening and clarification: I talk, you talk, and we each wait our turn. If what is said sounds like criticism, instead of clarifying this, the response might come back unusually harsh. This harsh tone gets an even harsher reply and off you go! The fire has been stoked and the original topic of discussion gets buried and perhaps never addressed. I can't emphasize the importance of clarifying someone's communication when there is a concern over criticism or anger.

A lot of communication goes awry because anger is assumed, but not intended, in the communication. Sometimes our communication can be pressured or impatient, which gives a false tone of being angry when this is not the case. This type of misunderstanding also occurs when people attempt to have a discussion that spans the entire house or between floors. Just raising our voice in an effort to be heard can give the false impression of an anger or negative intent. Again, the need to clarify your partner's intended message is a tool to avoid this type of conflict.

Another ineffective pattern of communication in

an exchange of anger occurs when we become impatient and have the expectation that others should understand and respond to us immediately. This pattern is conducive to mutual misunderstanding and the mistaken belief that a lack of immediate response is somehow a personal injustice. Clarifying questions in this pattern can often be viewed as annoying or impertinent and further fuel a person's anger. This pattern is a good example of how anger can be rooted in ego.

Another common source of friction in relational communication is misreading the tonal intent of the communication, which is important to aligning each person's perceptions so they are congruent with the experience and expectations.

Incongruence between words and behaviors can lead to misunderstanding and confusion. For some, an evening out for dinner might entail chicken wings and beer at the local pub. For others, an evening out might conjure up thoughts of a romantic opportunity of intimate conversation. These are different environments for each individual where the misunderstanding can cause an argument. What could have been a nice evening can easily erupt into a game of "he said, she said."

It is therefore important to be mindful of your tonal communication and intent when making plans. It is also important to be flexible about what you both expect. When communication and behavior are congruent in the planning stage, the resentment and hurt that comes with dashed expectations is less likely.

Adding Tools

To this point, we have taken an in-depth look at the nature of anger and its role in human suffering. We have seen how anger contributes to our suffering and the suffering of others. We have examined the question of whether you would rather add to the suffering of others or be the antidote to their suffering. Within this context, we've said that the path to uprooting your anger is by first learning to view other people through compassionate, selfless eyes.

We have also skimmed the surface of identifying how you contribute to the suffering of others and how this relates to your values. We have set goals and examined the distorted thinking that underlies your anger. Subsequently, you have established short- and long-term goals and a statement of intent that will guide your thoughts and behaviors toward goal attainment.

Now it's time to drill a little deeper into the specifics of your anger and both the triggers and patterns that are at its root.

What Triggers Your Anger?

Why is it that something or someone always seems to push our buttons? Why are the people closest to us most often the ones at the switch? And most importantly, why do certain people and events just seem to bring out our anger?

We all seem to have built-in triggers and responses. Some are healthy and some are not. If you were raised in Minnesota, as I was, the sight of new-fallen snow probably triggers feelings of playfulness and joy. However, at the same time, a frigid temperature without the snow sets off a desire to stay inside by the fire. Like the emotions they are tied to, we all have both positive and negative triggers, and we have to learn to cope with them.

In most cases, we are well aware of our anger triggers. Nevertheless, despite this awareness, we wander through life either hoping that people will not push our buttons, or we learn to avoid the anger stimulation as best we can. Unfortunately, these strategies rarely work, because life has a way of presenting us with challenges for growth.

Triggers usually have their roots in earlier life events and, when they occur, they can bring out a childlike response. Just like the firing pin on a bomb, something sets us off and we blow up or fall apart. I have learned over the years that it is important to understand our individual triggers so we can better anticipate them. I have also learned, however, that trying to keep life and other people from pushing our buttons is a futile effort.

Rather than trying to keep the world from pushing my buttons, it is more effective for me to focus on uprooting my buttons all together, leaving nothing for others to push.

For you to eliminate your anger buttons, you need to first identify them. While you are probably able to sit down and identify several causations, it is likely that you will have to view this exercise as a journal. When an event arises where you are triggered into anger, you can accurately add to the list.

Personal Exercise: Anger Triggers

What people, places or things trigger my anger?

Example: *I am triggered when my partner overspends on our credit cards.*

1. _______________________________________

____

____

2. _______________________________________

____

____

3. _______________________________________

____

____

4. ____
____
____

5. ____
____
____

Now that you have identified some of your anger triggers, take a moment to identify how you have been responding to these triggers.

How am I responding when my anger is triggered?

Example: *I confront her/him with the bill, I yell, we fight and I make financial threats.*

1. ____
____
____

2. ____
____
____

3. ____
____
____

4. ____
____
____

5. ____
____
____

Now that you have identified some of your responses, let's look at how you feel after these responses. In an effort to help you describe how you feel, I have included some examples below. You will notice that there are some positive feelings in this list, because it is important to acknowledge that sometimes the release of our anger can, in the short term, feel good:

Hopeless	Abandoned	Helpless
Useless	Hateful	Like a failure
Relieved	Empty	Obsessed with past mistakes
Sad	Guilty	
Anxious	Scared	Pain so deep it can't be fixed
Miserable	Angry	
Terrible	Tense	
Worthless	Sense of futility	Happy
Justified		Glad I said something
Tired	Burdened	
Irritable	As if I'm in hell	Empowered
Alone		

How does the response to my triggers make me feel?

Example: *I may feel some release, but mostly I feel frustrated and upset. I really don't like the fighting over this so often.*

1. ____

____

2. ____

____

3. ____

____

4. ____

____

5. ____

____

Now brainstorm some alternative responses for when you face an anger event. It is not only important to know what your triggers are, but you should also have an alternate plan of how to respond. These alternate responses can be broad, and may be as simple as "remove myself from the situation" or "take a time-out." Here are some other options.

Alternative responses for when I face my triggers.

Example: *I will wait until I am calm to speak about finances, and I will ask her/him when we can sit down and discuss our spending.*

1. ____

____

____

2. ____

____

____

3. ____

____

____

4. ____

____

____

5. ____

____

____

Physical Management of Anger

As mentioned earlier, I began to struggle with my own anger after ending my involvement with contact team sports. I then turned to martial arts to help fill the gap that had been created. In Chapter 3, we discussed how the uprooting of anger is much more complex, requiring a variety of tools and shifts in thinking. But management of physical well-being is an essential tool.

I want to be careful to not imply that playing contact sports is necessary, but rather that physical exertion itself is valuable in managing anger and overall health. It doesn't matter if you walk, bike, run, lift weights, dance or swing from a trapeze. If you want to maintain control over your anger and work toward its elimination, you must move your body. While less aerobic exercises certainly have their health benefits, I find that aerobic exertion, where the adrenaline gets pumping, is most effective in bleeding off the adrenaline that comes with anger.

Other physical activities such as gardening, yard work, painting, walking the dog and chopping wood are also useful activities that expel the energy associated with anger in healthy ways. I have clients who have painted their entire house (inside and out) and cut cords of wood to last several winters in an effort to redirect their anger. I even had a client who started her own dog-walking business because she walked her dog so frequently that she decided she should at least make some money.

When you are engaging in exercise as a tool to manage anger, it is important to focus on the exercise itself and not so much on the issue of anger. For example, hanging a punching bag in your basement can be a great tool for releasing your physical energy. However, if while punching the bag you envision pounding your boss and you cuss a blue streak, it's is not a good association.

I have seen this approach used with angry teenagers who were directed to simply expel their anger on the punching bag. The result was a conditioned response to pound things when they got angry. Inevitably, the punching bag approach led to real-life altercations that didn't work out well for anybody.

Therefore, if you are going to punch, chop, shoot or kick as a tool to manage your anger, be mindful of what you are doing and where your mind is. Focus on the task and on doing it correctly and safely. I have seen many wrists injured by people who flailed away at punching bags in anger. Talking through your anger with someone before or after exertion in an effort to disconnect the link between the activity and the anger is a beneficial strategy.

Nutrition

Individuals who struggle with issues of anger may want to consider limiting their intake of caffeine, energy drinks and stimulants. Caffeine and other stimulants that increase the heart rate and blood pressure tend to increase hypertension and move us just a bit closer to a state of hyper-arousal similar to anger. They serve to effectively close the gap between emotional arousal and our response.

This same philosophy applies to the use of alcohol, drugs or medications as a tool to manage anger. Alcohol is probably the worst coping tool for managing anger, yet it is one of the mostly widely used approaches. Using alcohol in an attempt to manage anger is a lose/lose situation. In some people, alcohol can serve as magnifying glass of their emotions. If anger is present, alcohol can quickly swing open the gates of emotion and unleash anger that might have normally been contained, especially if an individual has a great deal of sadness. Alcohol is a depressant and drinking it while angry, depressed or sad is like throwing gasoline on a fire. The result is explosive, it hurts, and the damage can last a long time.

While food can sometimes be comforting, it's not the best tool for managing anger either. When we turn to food as a source of comfort, we are usually craving carbohydrates or sugars. Chocolate is probably the all-time champion food of choice for comforting emotions. When we eat these foods, our body gets a kick of short-term energy that quickly runs out, leaving us with low energy, cravings for more, and feelings of guilt. In the long run, we put on weight, feel lethargic, and harbor self-criticism for letting ourselves go and having to buy new clothes.

A study is underway on the benefits of seafood on anger and violence. While most prisons are notorious for the poor quality of their cuisine and the violent behavior of their residents, they are ideal locations to test the hypothesis that violent aggression is largely a product of poor nutrition. Toward that end, researchers are studying whether inmates become less violent when put on a diet rich in vitamins and the fatty acids found in seafood. While no definitive results have been reported, research on the Omega 3 fatty acids associated with certain fleshy fish, such as salmon, has been effective in combating the low moods associated with depression. For this reason, I take Omega 3 fish oil supplements daily and it helps my mood, cholesterol levels and maybe even my anger.

There are many proven benefits to taking Omega 3 fish oil, including:

- Cardiovascular health

- Reduced inflammation

- Protection from stroke and heart attack

- Less depression and psychosis

- Reduction in breast, colon and prostate cancer

- Improved memory and recall

- Reduced incidence of childhood disorders

such as Attention Deficit

There is one food I can recommend for calming the emotions associated with anger: noncaffeinated teas, like chamomile, do have a calming effect. I have also found that some fruit blends, such as strawberry and orange, can have a calm and warming effect.

Distraction, Avoidance and Staying Busy

Staying busy, distracting ourselves, or otherwise avoiding our own anger or the anger of others are not effective coping tools. Staying busy by immersing ourselves in endless projects or by focusing our energies on other people, while productive, fails to address the need for working directly on the issue of anger. Ignoring it in this way won't improve it or make it go away. Anger is patient and insidious; failing to address it directly will only ensure that it rises to the surface again.

It's amazing how couples learn to distract themselves from their own anger or the anger of their partners. Like ostriches, we have an amazing capacity to stick our heads in the sand and ignore the damage that anger can cause.

There is a difference between avoiding anger and disengaging or taking a time-out when anger arises. One of the first tools for managing episodes of anger is to disengage by letting the other person know that you need time to think about the discussion or that you are not in a good place for having the discussion at the time. But people often make several mistakes with this strategy:

They simply leave the argument without verbalizing their own need to disengage.

They fail to acknowledge the importance of the issue to the other person.

They set the boundary and disengage, but do

nothing productive with this time-out, like going for a walk or talking with someone else (going out for a drink with the boys does not qualify).

They fail to set a time commitment for revisiting the issue.

Here is an example of effective disengagement and revisiting an issue between two people.

You know, clearly this is a hot topic and I really don't feel like getting into it now. Would you mind if I went for a walk and then got a good night's sleep? I've got some time before going to work tomorrow and I promise we can discuss this before I go.

Or

I apologize, but I haven't worked out in two weeks and just finished my third beer. Can we have this discussion when I'm more alert?

It can also be an effective strategy to acknowledge the importance of the issue to the other person and then ask for a time-out.

I know this is important to you, but I'm overwhelmed already and getting into this now would not be good. Can we make a commitment to talk about this after work tomorrow?

Or

This is too important for us to have this conversation over the phone. Can we discuss it in person tonight?

The Hostility Roadmap

Some people tend to be more logical in their thinking while others may be more emotional. The hostility roadmap can be an effective tool for developing a logical response to questions or situations that provoke anger.

Many of the strategies in this book are targeted

at creating a gap in our thinking and response so we don't fly off the handle with our destructive emotions. To effectively use the hostility roadmap, you really need to commit it to memory so you can mentally access it at any time. Initially you may want to duplicate this diagram on an index card to have with you until it becomes a part of your unconscious thinking, as we discussed previously, when counterbalancing your negative thoughts.

The process is simple. When in a provocative situation and your anger or cynicism presents itself, ask yourself, "Is this matter worth my continued attention?"

If not, disengage from it and move on. If you believe it is worth your attention, ask, "Am I justified?" Again, if you are not justified in this situation (if you are in the wrong or if it is really someone else's issue), disengage and move on.

If you are justified, ask yourself, "Do I have an effective response?" If you don't and your response will only add fuel to the fire, disengage and move on. If you do have an effective response, deliver it in a calm and compassionate tone. The goal here is to respond in such a way that others can truly hear you. Cynical responses and angry tones are the quickest ways to shut down the communication.

Personal Exercise: Cynical Thoughts, Anger, Aggression

Is this matter worth continued attention?   *Yes* ↓

Am I justified?———→ *No* (disengage)   *Yes* ↓

Do I have an effective response?—▶ *No* (disengage)

                         Yes ↓

Deliver your response in a calm, compassionate tone.

 # Chapter 8: Compassionate Strategies

It seemed rather incongruous that in a society of super sophisticated communication, we often suffer from a shortage of listeners. —*Erma Bombeck*

I love my work because I am always learning and trying to help others. The field of psychology and human performance offers a seemingly endless path of new theories and research. My work with clients is never redundant and, because I work with human beings, the challenges are always unique.

As you can see, uprooting anger necessitates a combination of philosophical understanding, cognitive shifts in thinking, movement toward true selflessness, and tools and strategies. One of the primary tools is to become a masterful communicator. An additional strategy covered in this chapter is in the power of forgiveness.

The Power of Human Language

Relational Frame Theory (RFT) is a research program that emphasizes the study of how the mind works (Hayes, Barnes-Holmes and Roche, 2001). This research suggests that many of the tools we use to solve problems actually lead us into traps that create human suffering. The basic premise of RFT is that human behavior is governed largely through networks of cognitive relations, which Hayes, Barnes, Holmes and Roche call relational frames. In other words, humans have the capacity to think relationally while nonhumans do not. We can relate objects in our environment to other objects in our environment, and we do so through our thoughts, feelings and behaviors. This ability to think relationally gives us the capacity to consciously analyze our environment and respond to it through language, art, tool making, music, building, etc.

While these relational frames are at the core of human thought, they are also at the core of human language. The written word is probably the best example of how we translate the relations we perceive into a symbolic representation of that thought. Our ability to link our relational thinking into verbal and expressive languages, and communicate this to others, is unique to human beings. This same ability can create the greatest misunderstanding and human suffering.

How we communicate, or how we fail to communicate, contributes more to anger than anything I can think of. Therefore, if the goal is to work toward uprooting your anger, it is essential to evaluate how your communication style and the styles of others contribute to your afflictive emotions.

Effective communication is all about conveying your messages to other people clearly and unambiguously. It is also about receiving information that others are sending to you with as little distortion as possible.

We have already discussed the tendencies of mental filtering that can occur through patterns of irrational thinking and how prolonged patterns of criticism can create a barrier of hearing criticism even when it is not present.

Effective communication involves effort from both the sender of the message and the receiver. It is a process frequently fraught with error, as messages are muddled by the sender or misinterpreted by the recipient. When this occurs, it can cause great confusion, wasted effort and missed opportunity. Communication is only successful when both the sender and the receiver understand the same information as a result of the communication.

By successfully getting your message across, you convey your thoughts and ideas effectively. When not successful, the thoughts and ideas you send do not necessarily reflect your thoughts or intent, causing a communications breakdown. These breakdowns create roadblocks that stand in the way of your goals and can be the source of irritability and anger.

The Art of Listening

People love nothing more than to know that they have been heard. This is an important lesson to understand in communication and in tempering afflictive emotions. The art of listening to others draws people closer and is the foundation of true understanding. Being overly talkative and/or verbose tends to push people away. The skill of listening is more conducive to social interest and usually ensures better understanding.

Notice how I have used the words "art" and "skill" to describe listening. I do so because listening can be difficult and it is a skill to be developed. While I was in school studying counseling and psychology, a lot of course work was placed on developing the skill of listening, and for good reason. How well you listen has a major impact on the quality of your relationships with others. Remember these guidelines as we discuss listening:

- Listen to obtain information.
- Listen to understand.
- Listen for enjoyment.
- Listen to learn.

Given the importance of listening, you would think people would be good at it, but most of us aren't. We retain on average a dismal 25-50% (depending on the source of the research) of what we hear. So, when you talk to your partner, friends, children, colleagues or employer for ten minutes, they only really hear two to five minutes of your words.

Turn the tables and you'll see that, when *we* are receiving directions or being presented with information, we aren't hearing the whole message either. We hope the important parts are captured in our 25-50%, but in many cases, they are not.

Clearly, listening is a skill we can all benefit from enhancing. By becoming a better listener, you can improve the clarity of a message, your productivity and your ability to influence others. You will also make great strides in avoiding conflict and misunderstandings.

The way to become a better listener is to practice "active listening," making a conscious effort to hear not only the words a person is saying but, more importantly, trying to understand the total message being sent. This is not as easy as it sounds. To do this, you must pay careful attention to the other person. I frequently conduct leadership training within organizations and the need for communications skills development is usually required. It is challenging work because truly listening and focusing in on what someone is saying and communicating takes some discipline.

To develop effective communication skills, you must not allow yourself to become distracted by what else may be going on around you. It is also important to stop forming counterarguments in your head that you will make when the other person stops speaking. Nor can you allow yourself to lose focus on what they are saying. All these barriers contribute to a lack of listening and understanding.

One method of increasing your focus and attention is to mentally repeat the words the speaker is saying as they say it. By engaging in this mental rehearsal, you will reinforce the person's message. This type of focus and rehearsal will also help you limit the degree to which your mind drifts to other topics.

Another way to enhance your listening skills is to let the other person *know* you are listening to what he/she is saying. Some clients tell me that they are constantly accused of not listening to people when they actually are. The problem in these situations is that they are not letting the other person know they have been heard. The technique of paraphrasing is guaranteed to assure others that you are listening.

Paraphrasing

Paraphrasing is done by waiting for the person to finish their sentence and then offering a short summary of what you heard in your own words. Paraphrasing is not a verbatim summary and should be no longer than one sentence. Paraphrasing is a powerful tool that can allow you to take control of communication because, in that moment, you are talking and the other person is listening. In fact, paraphrasing is the only technique I know of with which you can interrupt someone without appearing rude, because you are expressing interest in the other person's conversation. In their book, *Verbal Judo: The Gentle Art of Persuasion*, George J. Thompson, PhD, and Jerry B. Jenkins talk about the 14 Benefits of Paraphrasing:

1.   By paraphrasing, you have hooked the other person and got them listening.

2.   You've taken control because you're talking and they are listening.

3.   You're making sure of what you heard, right on the spot.

4.   If you haven't heard someone correctly, they can correct you.

5. You've made the other person a better listener.

6. You've created empathy.

7. You've gained their attention.

8. You can reduce "he said, she said."

9. Paraphrasing sounds like you're trying to *work* on the problem, rather than *reacting* to the problem.

10. Paraphrasing prevents metaphrasing or putting words into somebody's mouth.

11. You can ask others to paraphrase (reverse paraphrasing) what you said to clarify the conversation.

12. If you don't get communication right with your boss, you probably are not going to win later.

13. You establish the rules of engagement in a conversation in which others are almost forced to follow.

14. Paraphrasing is a rehearsal that etches the information in your mind.

Paraphrasing Stems:

Here are some examples of effective sentence stems that can be used for paraphrasing. Simply add a bit of what the other person has said and you will have a great paraphrase to ask for clarification:

What you're saying is ...?

Can you give me an example?

Help me understand this better.

Let me make sure I heard what you just said.

Let me be sure I heard that correctly

Let me ensure that we're on the same wavelength.

The beautiful thing about paraphrasing is that

summaries that are inaccurate or miss the mark do not usually offend people. When you paraphrase incorrectly, people may look at you a little funny, but they are glad you are making an effort to hear them. In these cases, people generally repeat, rephrase or clarify what they have said with no love lost, and then you paraphrase again. In some cases, I inaccurately paraphrase on purpose so the other person can crystallize their meaning or give me more information. Remember that you must *pay attention* to what the other person is saying in order for this to be effective!

To understand the importance of this, ask yourself if you've ever been engaged in a conversation in which you wondered if the other person was listening to what you were saying. You wonder if your message is getting across, or if it's even worthwhile to continue speaking. It feels like talking to a brick wall and it's something you want to avoid. The feeling of not being heard can be very personal.

The worst and most disrespectful way of showing that you are not listening is to check e-mails, send text messages, wear ear buds connected to your music device, or otherwise prioritize electronic gadgetry over interpersonal communication. In these circumstances, the message sent is clear and often two-fold: "Communicating with you is not that important to me" or "I am so important and busy that I don't have time for a one-on-one conversation with you." Neither of these messages is endearing or conducive to good communication.

Demonstrating that you are hearing what another person is saying doesn't always require a paraphrase. It can be as simple as a nod of the head or a simple "uh huh." You aren't necessarily agreeing with the person, you are simply indicating that you are listening. A slight nod of the head is a universal sign that you are trying to listen and is very effective for conveying your understanding. Offering a slight smile is also effective.

Body Language

Studies estimate that 80% of all communication is through body language and that only 20% is actually verbal. As human beings, we are tuned in, both consciously and unconsciously, to the body language of others. We have an innate ability to detect subtle communication in others and be in tune with circumstances in the world around us. We read people every day without even realizing it. We assess whether a person is good or bad, honest or dishonest. Reading a person comes naturally, but the problem is that most of us don't pay attention to the communication presented to us and therefore miss opportunities to be effective communicators. The result is misunderstanding, hurt feelings, frustration and sometimes anger.

An effective strategy to avoid frustration and communication breakdown is to physically attend to those you are speaking with and conduct yourself in an attentive manner. You can do this by:

• Removing all distractions.

• Turning off all electronics and not taking any calls.

• Sitting or standing squarely in front of the person you are speaking with and at the same eye level. Never stand over someone and expect an effective conversation.

• Removing physical barriers to communication such as desks or tables.

• Making eye contact and leaning in slightly to the person.

• Refraining from side conversations when you are in a group setting.

It is important to respond to the speaker in a

way that will encourage them to continue speaking and help you gain the information you need.

Active listening is a model for respect and understanding. Nothing is gained by emotionally attacking someone or interrupting their point. You are more likely to be given time for a counterargument in a conversation if you have allowed the other person to make their point. If you find yourself personalizing or wanting to respond emotionally to what someone has said, try to clarify their intent or meaning through paraphrasing.

As we discussed earlier, patience is an essential tool for learning to uproot anger, and it can be tested by our communication with others. Effective communication and active listening require concentration and focus. For most people, becoming a proficient listener is a matter of both unlearning old habits and learning new ones. Clarifying questions and good paraphrasing are skills. Once mastered, they can make communication more effective and easier. As difficult as the art of listening can be, it is like any skill. It takes work to learn at first, but becomes more fluent with time and practice. In the next chapter, we will discuss the concept of mindfulness—a practice that will directly support your work to become a masterful communicator.

Forgiveness

As long as our minds are captive to the memory of having been wronged, they are not free to wish for reconciliation with the one who wronged us.

—*Lewis B. Smedes*

In a time when peace is elusive and empathy is in short supply, the world is witnessing astonishing acts of forgiveness and of seeking forgiveness. On the global stage, Pope John Paul II made a comprehensive apology for the sins committed by the Roman Catholic Church and its members against groups of people throughout its history. In seeking forgiveness, the United States House of Representatives apologized to Black Americans, more than 140 years after slavery was abolished, for the "fundamental injustice, cruelty, brutality and inhumanity of slavery and Jim Crow" segregation. Prime Minister Tony Blair, of the United Kingdom, sought forgiveness for England's role in the Irish Potato Famine. His Holiness the Dalai Lama frequently speaks about his forgiveness of the Chinese government for atrocities committed against Tibet and its people.

On a personal level, there is evidence of forgiveness when couples make amends rather than separate. As part of their ninth step of recovery, people finding recovery from alcohol, drug, sex and gambling addictions by making direct amends to people they have harmed. Children forgive their parents almost instinctually and without reservation.

The importance of practicing forgiveness has been extolled for centuries by every religious tradition. Every time we witness an act of forgiveness, we marvel at its power to heal and its ability to eradicate hatred and conflict.

According to Gallup polls, forgiveness is something we all aspire to, and 94% of Americans surveyed said it was important to forgive. Unfortunately, only 48% said they usually tried to forgive others. Perhaps this is because forgiveness is something we don't fully understand. "Perhaps, as Friedrich Nietzsche thought, we associate forgiveness with weakness. Or perhaps we view forgiveness as an almost saintly quality that imbues only the very special and most certainly cannot be learned" (from a campaign for Forgiveness Research).

It is a myth that forgiving others is a weakness. In fact, those who have studied forgiveness say without qualification that forgiveness is actually a sign of strength. Research conducted by Stanford University's Campaign for Forgiveness Research, led by Dr. Carl Thoreson and his colleague, Dr. Fred Luskin, has shown that unresolved anger can be alleviated with the help of the age-old concept of forgiveness.

The last decade has produced much research on the many benefits of forgiving others, including:

• How letting go of anger and resentment can reduce the severity of heart disease and, in some cases, even prolong the lives of cancer patients.

• How forgiveness education could play a key role in reducing the vengeful responses that lead to criminal acts.

• How forgiveness can be an effective tool to help reconcile couples when other techniques have proved ineffective.

• How forgiveness can reduce anger and depression as well as enhance hopefulness and self-efficacy.

• How forgiveness can enhance existing interpersonal relationships.

Studies also suggest that forgiveness can be taught and learned. For our purposes, it is important to understand that forgiveness works directly on the emotion of anger (and related constructs such as resentment, hostility or hatred). Forgiveness diminishes the intensity and degree of anger within the mind and heart.

Steps toward Forgiveness

As I mentioned earlier, the concept of forgiveness has received a great deal of attention and research over the last decade. Thoreson and Luskin and Stanford's Campaign for Forgiveness Research have been at the forefront of not only understanding forgiveness, but of helping others move toward forgiveness.

Thoreson and Luskin define forgiveness as taking less personal offense, reducing anger, not blaming the offender, and developing increased understanding of situations that often lead to feeling hurt and angry. While forgiveness can be a liberating experience, it requires some focused effort and a conscious decision to actively forgive. Forgiving can be a difficult choice; I have worked with clients who were never able to move to a place of forgiveness.

The choice of whether to move toward forgiveness is often rooted in the ability to see how damaging hanging onto great hurt can be. Wouldn't it be nice to limit the times you are hurt or offended by others? To not get offended so often? To not get caught up in blaming others? Wouldn't it be nice if the act of forgiveness were never an issue? Like uprooting anger, forgiveness is a choice.

We can choose to suffer and add to the suffering of others or choose to not create our own suffering and contribute to the suffering of others.

According to Thoreson and Luskin, the process of forgiveness proceeds along four stages. The first is to acknowledge that you are filled with self-justified anger and that, at some point in your life, you have been hurt or wronged by someone. You blame that person for the pain you experience and say their actions are the cause of your anger. You have forgotten that you have a choice of how you are going to feel and forgiveness is not even a consideration. In this stage, there is both anger and sadness.

The second stage of working toward forgiveness begins when you start to realize that your anger does not feel good to you, or when you move to a place of wanting to repair the relationship because it is making you sick. In this stage, you are in a better place to view the problem from the other person's point of view, or you decide that it is time to just let go of the resentment you are carrying toward the other person, yourself or life. At this point, you are in a place to diminish your anger and forgiveness is possible.

The third stage is when you realize the benefits of forgiveness and make a choice to not attach your anger to past hurts. In this stage, people begin to make the connection between their inability to forgive and the decline in their physical and emotional well-being. Still, some struggle with wanting to address the issue of past harm and with a desire to repair the relationship. Others find contentment in their personal forgiveness and choose to move on without attempting reparation. At this stage, there is a personal discovery about the cost and benefit of holding onto anger and a conscious decision to hold onto hurt or to move on.

The fourth stage of forgiveness parallels our path of uprooting anger and involves a proactive choice to not get angry. At this point, the choice of forgiveness is present consciously and subconsciously. Forgiveness occurs in advance of the triggers we face and may involve these types of thoughts:

• I'm not going to waste my time getting frustrated and angry. I can forgive myself, others, life and God.

• I've felt the hurt when others have not forgiven me and I don't want to contribute to that.

• I'm not going to allow this to sidetrack me from the beauty of life.

• Everyone faces a certain degree of suffering and I've made the choice to not add to it.

The four stages of forgiveness and uprooting anger both require a humble and selfless approach to life. In my own self-interest, I can choose to be angry and hold onto resentments or I can choose not to. The four stages of forgiveness are unique to every individual, just as their relationship to others and the world is unique. Therefore, these stages may not follow the same order and time frame from one person to the next. Like anger, forgiveness is a personal choice to embrace healing for ourselves and others.

Chapter 9: Mindfulness and Meditation

Cultivation to the mind is as necessary as food to the body.
— *Marcus Tullius Cicero*

The most important lessons I've learned about uprooting anger are that there is no one magic cure and that it is an ongoing and active process. I have a toolbox of core strategies that keep me growing and moving toward uprooting anger and they have become integrated into my life's routine. However, as with many things in life, routines can change and, consequently, so will the outcome. For example, during those times when I fail to work out regularly or practice meditation, I soon notice a shift in my mood. Patterns of impatience will begin to leach through the surface of my everyday interactions with great subtlety.

Like relapse of any kind, the symptoms of slipping into old patterns often seem to sneak up on us. In truth, they rarely sneak up on us. The symptoms are evident; we just fail to pay attention to them. Because of the invisible nature of relapse or reoccurrence of old patterns, it is important to regularly integrate coping strategies that target an attentive focus on ourselves. Practices that help us routinely take our own pulse can be the difference between success and failure when it comes to managing our emotions.

In learning to manage my own anger and that of clients, I've discovered two essential practices for uprooting and eliminating anger. They have been a part of my growth in anger management and are an extension of psychology, Buddhism and Eastern philosophy. These two practices are mindfulness and meditation.

Mindfulness

To be successful in uprooting anger from your life, you must cultivate a mindset of living life in every moment. Too often, we are guided by our experiences of the past or old patterns of distorted thinking. There is great benefit to living life in the present, as if each moment is of value even if it contains sadness or fear. This owning of life, each moment and every experience, is called mindfulness.

In a world where we are bombarded daily with an unending stream of demands and information, the need for developing the discipline to create our own mental calm is a valuable skill. If our goal is to uproot anger and view the world from a more positive lens, the challenge is more difficult because we continually face a barrage of violent and heartbreaking images from multiple media sources.

Mindfulness is a core tenet of Buddhist meditation and has flourished for 2,500 years in both monastic and secular worlds. The practice of mindfulness and meditation has spread its roots throughout the world, as Eastern teachers have brought their knowledge and practices to the West, along with other practices such as yoga, tai chi and martial arts. Increasingly, the benefits and need for mindfulness meditation practices have given rise to greater research and openness toward their use. Because the benefits of mindfulness practice is rooted in self-inquiry and understanding, it is a technique for managing anger that stands on its own and is independent of any belief system or ideology.

Mindfulness can be best described as a particular way of paying attention. It is not just about how we pay attention to the world, but also about how we pay attention to ourselves. As we have discussed, a key component to uprooting anger is to pay attention to what we are thinking, how we are responding to the world, and how we are impacting those around us. Mindfulness can help all these areas and create a gap between our anger and the negativity that surrounds so much of our lives.

Mindfulness is difficult because it can be elusive. Life is complex and there are so many things to be mindful of that it's easy to lose our way and get caught in the trap of just getting through each day. Rather than living life, we are caught up in simply surviving life. Like the other steps in this book, the practice of mindfulness will not do you much good if you simply read it, do a few exercises and then forget about it. The goal of mindfulness, as with overcoming anger, is to pay attention to the events in your life without being judgmental or defensive.

The ultimate tool to help develop mindfulness is the practice of meditation. Meditation requires that you set aside a specific time for daily practice, but you can cultivate mindfulness throughout the day. Here are some exercises you can do to help you begin to tune yourself to a mindful frequency.

Personal Exercises: Enhancing Mindfulness

The 60-Second Raisin: Sit down with some raisins. Pop one into your mouth and eat it as you normally would. Then take a second raisin and place it in front of you. Examine it. Make note of its size and texture. Take out another raisin and put the two next to each other. Examine the differences in their size and patterns of the wrinkles.

Now, pick up one raisin and feel its texture as you roll it around in your fingers. Bring the raisin to your nose and see if you can detect its smell (caution: don't snort the raisin). Close your eyes and gently place the raisin inside your mouth and roll it around with your tongue. Feel the texture and the initial hint of sweetness. Do this for at least thirty seconds and don't begin to chew it until you are ready. Slowly begin to chew the raisin and pay attention to the taste and how the sweetness activates your taste buds. Notice what parts of your mouth react and how your saliva begins to flow. Continue to chew the raisin slowly and completely for another thirty seconds until it becomes a liquid in your mouth. Gently swallow and pay attention to the feeling of it sliding down your throat and the lingering flavor in your mouth. Now answer these questions:

Did the second raisin taste different from the first? How?

____

____

____

What does the raisin feel like in your mouth when you savor it and pay attention to the texture?

____

____

____

How does it feel as it begins to break down and become liquid?

____

____

____

How does it feel sliding down your throat?

____

____

____

Was there a difference between eating the raisin mindfully and the way you usually eat a raisin?

____

____

____

Mindful Tea Drinking: Start to boil a pot of water and place a tea bag or a tea ball filled with tealeaves into a cup. Slowly pour the boiling water into the cup. Notice the steam rising from the cup and feel the heat. Pay attention to the floating of the tea bag and the change of the water's color. While the tea steeps, gently clasp your hands around the outside of the cup without touching it and notice the warmth. Test the cup to see if it's too hot to touch.

If not, fully clasp the cup and notice the warmth. Notice the darkness of the tea.

Now bring the cup up near your lips and breathe the tea's aroma. Blow gently across the top of the tea and notice it ripple and see the steam dissipate. Now take a sip and make a note of the taste and warmth as it run down your throat. Relax and take in the experience, then gently set the cup down. Describe your experience below:

Describe the overall warmth of the experience.

____
____
____
____

What does the tea smell like?

____
____
____

Was the tea initially too hot to drink?

____
____
____

What does tea taste like?

____
____
____

Do you feel warmer than when you began? ____________

Mindful Eating (You may want to try this while eating a meal alone at first to avoid outside distractions.)

When you are nearing mealtime, take a moment to wash your hands, not only as an act of hygiene, but also as a means of cueing your mind to your inner eating experience. Take an empty plate and prepare moderate portions of food with the knowledge that you can always come back for more.

As you approach the table, take in the aromas, textures and colors of the food. Transition your mind from the cares of the day and envision this meal as a private time to enjoy and reenergize yourself.

Instead of digging into the meal like a lumberjack, sit down and intentionally pause for a moment. Take three deep relaxing breaths, filling your lungs slowly and completely. Make your exhales twice as long as your inhales.

Now pick up your utensil, take a moderate-sized bite, and place your utensil down. Chew slowly and thoroughly between bites. Pay attention to the tastes, aromas and textures that each bite offers. Swallow each bite and follow it with a gentle sip of your beverage. During your meal, periodically evaluate the flavors and tastiness of the food.

Being this attentive to a meal is unnatural at first, but research shows that relishing our food enhances not only the experience of the meal, but also our sense of being full. When we pay attention to our eating, there is a tendency to eat less because we detect the gustatory sensations that often go unnoticed.

After the meal, describe your experience below:

What particular thoughts came up during the meal?

____

____

____

Did you become impatient?

____

____

How does it feel to eat alone?

____

____

____

Where did you mind wander to during the meal?

____

____

____

Did you discover some new flavors that you had previously overlooked?

____

____

____

Did you make note of whether the meal was a healthy one for you or not?

____

____

____

Because we generally eat several times a day, mindful eating is an excellent way to stay in contact with the present moment and make the most of this time.

Mindful Walking: Developing mindfulness is about being in the moment during our day-to-day routines and there are, therefore, many opportunities to practice:

If you are doing the dishes, do only the dishes and pay attention.

When you are talking with your children, put down the Blackberry and have a mindful conversation.

Instead of taking the elevator, take the steps and count how many there are.

One simple way of creating awareness in your life is to practice mindful walking. We walk every day, and most of us should probably walk more often. Mindful walking differs from a regular walk in that the goal is to pay attention to the actual experience of walking. As you can guess from the experiences in mindfully eating a raisin or drinking tea, exercises in mindfulness are not as simple as they appear. This is true for mindful walking because we are usually walking for a reason or with our minds crowded with thought. Most often, people walk with the thought of where they would like to be and don't focus on where they are or what they are doing. Few people actually walk today without being connected to some type of personal device to feed them a stream of music or conversation.

Walking mindfully requires that you pay attention to the experience of walking: the sensation of moving and of each step. Focus on the act of heal-toe strides and the shifting of your body weight. Walk silently through the entire walk and pay attention to where your mind goes without purposefully directing your thought.

When you're walking mindfully, the goal is not to specifically walk somewhere or for a certain period of time or at a certain pace. You can walk slowly at first, then walk more quickly. It is enough just to be present, in the moment, taking each step one at a time. One method of enhancing this focus is to walk in a circle or back and forth in a line. This rhythmic pattern of walking helps calm the mind because you are not going anywhere and your distractions become more limited. Of course, our thoughts may get distracting and you may find the whole idea of walking nowhere stupid or annoying. These moments will challenge you to really focus your thinking and counterbalance your negativity.

While the initial practice of mindful walking might be with a focus on your feet, body and the act of walking itself, you can gradually expand your focus to a mindfulness of what in your environment draws your attention. Take time to observe the patterns in the clouds and trees. Watch the sunlight dance on the water and file these images away to draw on during a day's hectic moments.

The most important part of mindfulness practice is to continually incorporate it into your life. While these initial practices may bring a sense of calm and focus that is enjoyable, it's easy to be swept back up into a routine of helter-skelter living. Mindfulness practices are helpful in developing the focus and awareness required to intervene on patterns of anger and destructive emotions. Each moment of mindful being is a moment that becomes part of your life and will contribute to your movement beyond anger.

Meditation Practices: Visualization

I was introduced to the practice of visualization when I was a high-school athlete. Tennis was one of the first sports to introduce the practice of visualization into its training curriculum. Visualization is also called guided imagery, mental rehearsal, meditation, and a variety of other things. No matter the term, the basic techniques and concepts are the same. Generally speaking, visualization is the process of creating a mental image or intention of what you want to happen or feel.

In tennis, visualization was the creation of a mental picture of moving toward the ball and visualizing the stroke and placement of my shot. As a goalie in hockey, visualization was helpful in maintaining my focus and for clearly seeing the puck as it traveled through traffic. As a skydiver, visualization helps me prepare for jumps. (It is helpful in mentally slowing down the entire process, because things happen very quickly in freefall and mistakes can be rather unforgiving.)

Athletes use the practice of visualization to "intend" an outcome of a race or training session. Visualization as a form of meditation is also used by athletes to simply rest and generate a feeling of calm and focus. By imagining a scene, an image of a past performance or a future desired outcome, the athlete is taught to simply "step into" that feeling. The athlete imagines the detail and the way it feels to perform in the desired way. It has always made sense to me that, if I can't *imagine* success, I am unlikely to be able to *produce* success.

For visualization to really work, you not only have to see what it is you want to achieve, but you must apply your positive mind and truly believe that you will achieve it. With effective visualization, you can cultivate a sense of confidence that what you are imagining will actually come to pass. The technique of visualization can also be applied to real-life situations such as public speaking, interviewing, difficult conversations and illness.

The practice of visualization can also be a powerful tool for managing anger, and I frequently rely on one particular image to help me. I remember the time I lost my temper with my daughter when she was just a young child. I don't even recall the circumstances, but I do remember how my explosion of anger shattered my little girl. I will never forget how my anger blew right through her and left her with absolute fear. In that moment, there was nothing left and she was too young to know what to do. In that moment, I failed to think about the power I have as a person or a father. It was my anger and it was about my letting it out. My daughter's tears, hyperventilation, trembling and fear quickly led me to realize that I never wanted to do that again to her or any other person. As humbling as it is, I frequently take my mind back to that moment and allow myself to see the image of my frightened child and feel the sadness of that moment. When I visualize this, it reinforces my goal of never wanting to do that again.

Personal Exercise: Sadness

Take a moment and think of a time when your anger harmed someone else. Visualize every detail of how you acted and how the other person looked and felt. As painful as it might be, allow yourself to feel the sadness attached to the pain this incident caused. Once you have a clear image of this moment, write out all the details and include the feelings attached to this incident:

____

____

____

____

____

____

____

____

Now hold this image in your mind and write a vow or mantra that you can attach to this image as a tool for course correction whenever you feel out of control with your anger.

Example: *I will never unleash my anger on others again and will strive to treat everyone with kindness and compassion.*

____

____

____

____

____

____

____

____

____

Traditional Meditation

When I began to study martial arts, my meditation practice began to expand beyond visualization and an application to sports. Meditation became a tool for physical and mental management of life and anger. Over the last twenty years, my personal practice has grown, just as the practice of meditation has integrated itself into modern life. Meditation is now a much more familiar word in our vocabulary. Psychologists and other health and healing professionals now endorse meditation as a tool for relieving stress, maintaining health and promoting creative thought. A great deal of research is also being conducted on the physical, mental and emotional benefits of meditation, including its ability to:

• Lower oxygen consumption.

• Decrease respiratory rates.

• Increase blood flow and slow the heart rate.

• Increase exercise tolerance in heart patients.

• Lead to a deeper levels of relaxation.

• Reduce blood pressure.

• Reduce anxiety attacks by lowering the levels of blood lactate.

• Decrease pain due to tension and headaches.

• Build self-confidence.

• Increase serotonin production, which influences mood and behavior. Low levels of serotonin are associated with depression, obesity, insomnia and headaches.

• Help in chronic diseases like allergies and arthritis.

• Reduce premenstrual syndrome.

• Help in postoperative healing.

• Enhance the immune system. Research has revealed that meditation increases the activity of "natural-killer cells" that kill bacteria and cancer cells.

• Reduce activity of viruses and emotional distress.

The word *meditation* is used in a variety of ways

and some clients still look at me crossways when I mention meditation as a coping tool. So confusion remains about what mediation is and how it is practiced. Some people mistakenly use the word *meditate* to mean thinking or contemplating your navel. Others view meditation as daydreaming, fantasizing or some new-age practice. And still others view meditation as a religious practice that may conflict with their own.

The root word of meditation, *medi*, is similar to the root word for medical or medicate. The root meaning of *medi* is to "attend to" or "pay attention to" something. Meditation practice is as old as humanity and has its roots in many religious practices. It has always been a mainstream practice in the East, and Western religions are beginning to reintegrate their meditative past. Meditation is described in ancient Hindu texts dating back to the Vedic traditions 2000-3000 years ago.

Buddha, Prince Siddhartha Gautama, achieved enlightenment through meditation practice in 588 BC. In the second century AD, Christian monks, known as the Desert Fathers, retreated from the world to live in simplicity and meditate in an effort to get closer to God. Kabalistic (Jewish) meditation is one of the most ancient ways of communing with God. The Muslim tradition of Sufism has also long incorporated meditation practice into its religious rituals. Meditation is not some sort of strange or foreign practice that requires you to change your beliefs, your culture or your religion.

Meditation is also not a form of hypnosis or autosuggestion that attempts to program, manipulate or control the mind. Meditation is a specific technique for completely resting the mind and attaining a state of consciousness that is totally different from our normal waking state. In meditation, we are fully awake but our mind is not focused on the "to do" lists of life and the world around us. Instead, the mind is clear, relaxed and focused "within." While the practice of mediation might seem pretty simple, it is a discipline that can be very hard to master.

In a simplistic way, I like to think of meditation as a practice for strengthening and disciplining my brain and thought processes. Sort of like an exercise in mental pushups. The greatest challenge in meditation practice is overcoming what a teacher of mine liked to call "monkey mind." Monkey mind is what you notice when you sit still, breath and try to calm your thinking. When you do this, especially when you are first trying to meditate, you will notice how your mind jumps from thought to thought like monkeys in a tree. Sometimes people have a lot of monkeys in their tree and they can be very active.

The goal of meditation is to find a point of focus, like your breath, as a means of getting the monkeys to calm down, get out of the tree and sit quietly. Other types of focus can include a visual focal point or a mantra or an analytical thought. It is at this very point, when the monkeys are jumping around, that people first struggle with the practice of meditation. In our supercharged society, many people lack the patience and discipline required to calm their monkeys. I have had clients who became overwhelmed at this point because they noticed the sadness or negativity of their thoughts.

Meditation practice is an essential tool if the goal is to uproot anger. Meditation is a discipline that helps create the gap we have discussed, which is helpful for delaying our response to anger. Meditation is a process, and you will learn several things as you become more fluent in your practice:

- How to relax your body.

- How to sit in a comfortable and steady position.

- How to calm your breathing.

• How to witness the thoughts traveling in your mind (monkeys).

• How to evaluate these thoughts and either attach or detach from them.

• How not to allow yourself to become disturbed by your thinking or situations that arise.

Meditation and Diaphragmatic Breathing:

Preparation: Preparation and a certain consistency in your meditation practice will have great benefits in training your mind. Here are some suggestions:

Create a place to practice. Ideally, practice in the same place each time you meditate.

Find time to practice. Try to practice at the same time during the day or evening. Plan for this time and reduce all distractions. Take the phone off the hook, close the door, let your family know not to disturb you, etc.

Wear comfortable clothing. Remove constraining items such as watches, glasses and shoes.

Take care of your hygiene. Go to the bathroom before practicing and try not to practice 2-3 hours after a meal. Avoid caffeine.

Stretch your muscles from top to bottom before you start.

Try to meditate for a minimum of thirty minutes a session. It will generally take at least ten minutes to quiet the mind and get the monkeys to calm down.

Allow no excuses. Initial practice means that you are in what I call the "Nike phase of training"—you simply "must do it" even if you don't feel like it. You will begin to look forward to this time and become protective of it.

Positioning: Sit in a chair with your feet on the floor and your spine straight, or sit cross-legged on the floor. When sitting on the floor, try putting a pillow just under your hips to help your spine remain straight and keep you from slouching. It is important that you sit in a position that keeps your head, neck and trunk aligned so you can breathe freely and diaphragmatically. Sitting against a wall or the back of a chair will help keep your back straight and give you support. However, don't become dependent on this position or your back muscles will not get stronger. You may begin with this support, but gradually try to do without it or stick with sitting in a good upright chair.

Close your eyes, let your facial muscles relax, and gently close your mouth without any tension in your jaw. Your arms should be completely relaxed with hands resting gently on your knees.

Hands: There are several universal positions for the hands in meditation, and you can choose the one that is most comfortable for you. All these positions have the same thing in common: They are in some way closed to keep your internal energy flowing within you. Your chosen hand position will also become a natural trigger for relaxation and calm that you can use in any situation.

Gently join the thumb and index finger of each hand.

Place your right hand inside your left and gently touch your thumbs together.

Bring your hands together in a "prayer" position.

Although less traditional, I have many clients who like to hold their hands with their finger tips together.

Diaphragmatic Breathing: The diaphragm is located just above your stomach and in line with the lowest rib on your rib cage. It is from this point that you will draw breaths in and push breaths out of your body. If you are just beginning, you may want to place your right hand on this spot to help your focus. As you breathe from your diaphragm, you should feel your hand expand out as you draw in a breath and contract inward as you exhale.

Try to breathe in and out through your nose. This helps to slow down and lengthen your breaths and keeps your mouth from getting too dry.

As you position yourself, close your eyes, and begin breathing, focus on these three things:

1. Strive to make your breathing silent. If you can hear yourself breathe, you are probably breathing too hard.

2. Make your inhaling breath and your exhaling breath of equal length (balanced) and smooth. At first, you may want to count along with your inhalations and exhalations so that they become equal. Strive for smooth silent breaths.

3. Do not hold your breath at the peak of inhalation or when exhaling. Smoothly transition from your inhalation to exhalation. Pausing can disrupt your natural rhythm.

Surveying Your Body: As you begin your meditation, mentally survey and observe your body. Once you are positioned and breathing correctly, begin this systematic survey of your body from the crown of your head down to your toes. Let there be no tension in your forehead, in your cheeks and jaw, in your neck and shoulders and from your arms to your fingertips.

Mentally return to the shoulders, allowing no tension. Let there be no tension in the chest. Let go. Do not make suggestions to your body, but rather survey it. Let your attention move to the abdominal area. Survey the pelvic area and hips, thighs, knees, calves, ankles, feet and toes.

Now return to the crown of your head and begin to visualize your body again. If you discover an area that has an ache or a pain, quietly guide your mind to that spot and imagine your mind and breathing healing that area. Do not doubt that your mind can heal such discomfort.

Some Goals for Your Meditation: Meditation means "focused attention," and you can view the process of meditation as a form of mind training. Part of the process of your meditation will be to move from a "monkey mind" to a "quiet mind." In meditation, our focused attention is in contrast to the scattered, distracted state of mind that we often have throughout the day.

As you begin to breathe, you may notice your mind racing from thoughts of work, family, your health, etc. (noisy mind). Be patient and focus on the previously described aspects of breathing. Begin by doing the above exercise for fifteen minutes a day. In time, you will notice a transformation of quietness in both your mind and body when you meditate. Increase the length of time you meditate, as you feel comfortable.

Closing Your Meditation: When ending your meditation session, before you open your eyes, take time to thank yourself for the time you have spent. This is also a good time to pray or engage in a private moment of spiritual worship if you wish.

As you finish, slowly raise your hands to your eyes and rub them gently (not if you are wearing contact lenses). Like closing your eyes is a signal for your body to relax, a gentle rub is a signal for your body to awaken.

Do not stand up immediately! Take your time and stretch your legs, move to one knee and slowly bring yourself to a standing position. If you end your meditation in a rush and quickly stand up, you are undoing some of your accomplishments. Standing too quickly may also cause a shift in blood pressure and dizziness.

Guidelines and Goals for the First Month: The first one or two months of your meditation practice should be devoted to attaining a still, comfortable posture. Steadiness of posture means that you are able to sit still and keep the head, neck and trunk aligned. Allowing your posture to become comfortable means that you are not uneasy or cramping in any way. If you are sitting on a cushion to meditate, it should be neither too high nor too hard, and you avoid using a spongy, unsteady cushion.

For the first month, you may use the support of a wall or chair to help you tell when you are keeping your head, neck and trunk in a straight line. After that, learn to sit independently of such support. A firm meditation seat can be made from a wooden plank or board covered with two blankets folded into quarters.

At the first level of practice, obstacles may arise on several dimensions: First, the body may shake, sway, perspire or become numb. Next, the subtler muscles such as cheeks or eyes may twitch. You should learn to be patient and ignore all this. Like any new learning, the body may rebel when you try to discipline it.

If your throat gets dry while you are meditating, you can take a few sips of water. In certain cases, you may notice that there is excessive saliva in your mouth. Both of these symptoms may be indicators of overeating or consuming bad food.

You may also notice that your feet or legs fall asleep. When this happens, simply extend that limb until the numbness stops. Eventually, you will want to focus on the numb leg and, through mental imagery, direct the flow of blood down your leg to stop the tingling feeling.

When you begin to meditate, you should not try

to sit for a long time. To start, 15-20 minutes will be sufficient. Every third day you can expand your practice by three minutes until your meditation time is between 30-40 minutes. Gradually, when your posture becomes steady, the time will easily extend itself. Developing a still, steady posture will bring you great joy. Discomfort is not a good sign. Massage your toes, legs, thighs and eyes with your hands when you get up from your meditation.

When closing your meditation with a prayer or positive affirmation, make sure to pray for the strength of your meditation practice and give thanks for taking the time to practice. Selfish prayers feed the ego and can weaken us. Try not to make your prayer and meditation ego-centered.

Guided Imagery

As mentioned, meditation takes consistent practice in order for you to benefit. Many clients who aspire to meditate struggle most with making time to practice and with the frustration of calming the mind. Many of the research studies on the benefits of meditation practice have found that the amount of time spent in meditation directly correlates to the success of the study, so researchers have looked for options to improve the time spent in meditation. Recorded guided imagery CDs have proved to be an effective tool for helping people learn meditation practice and overcome the obstacles of time and monkey mind. I frequently recommend a series of CDs by Jon Kabat-Zinn as excellent guided imagery tools: www.mindfulnesscds.com.

While guided imagery is often performed first by listening to a CD, I have found that once I have been exposed to a guided journey, I can usually perform this on my own when I desire. Here is a script for guided meditation that you can begin with.

As you reach a state of "quiet mind" and calm in

your breathing, begin to imagine yourself in a beautiful, natural place. This sanctuary can be a place from your imagination or a place where you have been before—on top of a mountain, by the ocean, in a field of flowers, in a forest or meadow. In your mind's eye, begin to imagine yourself as actually being in this place right now.

Begin to use all your senses to clarify the image and reality of being in this sanctuary:

What smells are there (sweetness of flowers, salty breezes)?

What do you see (color of the water, flowers, trees, sunlight)?

What sounds do you hear (ocean waves, the songs of birds, a gentle breeze)?

Are you experiencing any tastes (dryness, saltiness, thirst)?

What do you feel? Look up at the sun and feel its warmth. Feel the breeze across the hairs of your arms. Feel the softness of the sand or ground beneath you.

Like an artist, paint a canvas in your imagination of a beautiful natural sanctuary that you can return to any time you wish in your meditation. Enjoy the peacefulness of this place until you are ready to either visualize a goal or end your meditation session.

If you choose to end your session, simply look over your sanctuary and commit the details to memory. Imagine drifting above this place and viewing the image from that viewpoint. Slowly drift away from your sanctuary, returning your focus to your breathing technique. End your session as you normally would.

Deep Muscle Relaxation: Deep-muscle relaxation training consists of tensing and releasing various muscle groups throughout the body while practicing diaphragmatic breathing techniques. This exercise is conducive to stress release and is incompatible with anxiety and anger. It is also an effective technique for relaxing the body and inducing sleep. An essential part of learning how to relax involves learning to pay attention to the feelings of tension and relaxation in your body.

This exercise employs tension to produce relaxation. The initial production of tension is required so that, when we release the tension, deep relaxation is the result. Like anything else, this requires practice.

Preparation: Prepare yourself as you would with your regular meditation practice and in your usual place for meditation. Unlike the seated meditation you usually practice, deep muscle relaxation is done lying flat on the floor or bed with your spine straight or sitting upright in a chair.

Steps to Inducing Relaxation: Position yourself, close your eyes and begin diaphragmatic breathing and your meditation induction techniques. Continue meditation for about ten minutes.

Curl your toes toward the arches creating tension in your feet. Hold this tension for 10-15 seconds, take a deep breath in, and release the tension in your feet as you exhale slowly. Imagine all your tension flowing out through your toes as you wiggle them slightly.

Create tension in your calf muscles (you my want to point your feet upward). Hold this tension for 10-15 seconds, take a deep breath, exhale, and release the tension as you relax slowly.

Create tension in your butt (gluteus maximus) muscles, feeling yourself rise up from your chair or position. Hold this for approximately 20 seconds, as this is a large muscle group. Take a deep breath, exhale, and release the tension as you relax slowly.

Draw your stomach muscles in as if to touch

your backbone, creating tension in your stomach muscles. Hold this for 10-15 seconds. Take a deep breath, exhale, and release the tension as you relax slowly.

Roll your shoulders forward slightly, bearing down on your chest (pectoral) muscles. Hold this for 20 seconds, as this too is a larger muscle group. Take a deep breath in, exhale, and release the tension as you relax slowly.

Slowly raise your shoulders toward your ears, creating tension in your neck and shoulder muscles. Hold this for 10-15 seconds. Take a deep breath in, exhale, and release the tension as you relax slowly. Slowly roll your head as if looking left, then back right. Return your head to a centered position.

Gradually ball each hand into a fist and begin to squeeze. Add the tension of your forearms and upper arms (biceps) until your entire arm is tense. You may experience a slight quiver and warmth in your hands and arms. Hold this for 20 seconds. Take a deep breath in, exhale, and release the tension as you relax slowly. Wiggle your fingers slightly and visualize all your tension flowing out the tips of your fingers. Return your arms to a comfortable position.

Shut your eyes tightly, creating muscle tension around the eyes, forehead and cheeks. Pull the corners of your mouth back tightly. Basically, make a funny face by creating tension in the facial muscles. Hold this for 10-15 seconds. Take a deep breath in, exhale, and release the tension as you slowly relax. In this stage, do not clench your teeth or try to create tension in the jaw.

Now review the condition of each of each muscle group and visualize them becoming more relaxed. You may notice your torso becoming heavy and your palms becoming warmer. These effects are indicators of deep-muscle relaxation.

Lie quietly for several moments while maintaining your diaphragmatic breathing. At this time, you may wish to remain quiet, go to sleep, practice visualization, or focus on a goal.

Before opening your eyes, slowly raise your hands and rub your eyes gently. When ready, sit up slowly and stretch a little before slowly standing.

Managing Anger and Cultivating Patience

Hatred and anger impair the practice of meditation. Meditation on anger and patience is a more advanced technique called "analytical meditation practice." The goal is to look at anger and patience from a variety of angles during meditation and try to come up with solutions.

Analytical Meditation I: The preliminary practice of this analytical meditation is an extension and integration of several exercises you have worked on in earlier parts of this book. This meditation involves focusing on the negative aspects of not having patience or of having hatred and intolerance toward others. In the first part of this meditative state, you want to take time to reflect on the impact your anger has had on you and others. Create a mental image and allow yourself to get uncomfortable with your images of anger.

The second part of this mediation is to shift your mental focus to the benefits of having greater patience and tolerance. We have also laid the foundation for this practice in earlier exercises. Focus this second part of your meditation on images of calm and patience in situations or triggers of anger. This meditation is a powerful reminder of where you have been and where you would like to be. It is a mental rehearsal of your commitment to not uproot your anger.

Analytical Meditation II: While meditating, imagine an enemy or person of dislike in front of you and the consequences of responding with anger to this person. You can choose a potential enemy, person or situation that irritates you. Everyone has this type of acquaintance or interaction with someone.

Bring this person or moment into focus.

Think about the situations that could arise from negative interactions with this person.

- This person may hurt you.
- This person may hurt your family.
- This person may begin using bad language.
- This person may hurt you in material terms.

At this point, you may begin to feel anger while thinking about the potential results of anger.

Now begin to focus beyond just the person or situation. Visualize the situations this person may be experiencing in their lives and how this may cause them to act in an angry way. Try to imagine the permutations of their suffering and visualize their negative thoughts or day's events that are potentially fueling their anger.

This person may have just been fired from work, or found out their child is sick, or have an emotional illness. Visualize how these negative events may be influencing their eruption of anger. See how they may be no longer independent of their anger and may be overpowered by hate. Consider the external agents that may be influencing them. Contemplate on how he or she may have a mental illness and how inappropriate it may be to retaliate. Remember that a mad person may not be crazy, but a person who responds to the mad person probably is.

As you reflect on these situations and create an awareness of this other person's anger, you may notice that your feelings of anger begin to lessen or fade. To a certain degree, you may begin to feel compassion for this individual as you focus on their suffering.

Managing Resentment, Old Anger, Grudges

This technique, as with most good things, takes time. As we discussed in the section on forgiveness, holding a grudge for past harms only continues to hurt you and your relationships in the present. This exercise may enhance your determination to let go and reinforce your earlier work on forgiveness.

If someone in your past has done you harm, you have probably wasted energy on your anger and hatred toward this person. You have probably given little thought to the deluded thoughts and afflictive conditions of this individual. In this meditation practice, the focus is not on the person who harmed you, but on the situations and deluded thinking that plagued the person who harmed you. There is a conscious effort to stop focusing on the person or tool of harm and start focusing on the underlying delusion and suffering of the other person.

Using the same analytical technique as before, visualize an image of a past hurt or a person who has hurt you. Meditate on the potential suffering of this incident. Visualize the continuing suffering that will exist if you seek revenge or retaliate. Meditate on the potential causes that have "forced" this person to respond with anger. Try to see this situation in an enlightened way and do not generalize or catastrophize the gravity of this situation.

Ask yourself if this suffering is something that can be resolved; if so, focus on a solution much like you did with the Hostility Road Map on Pages 109-110. Don't worry about or attach emotion to it. Become calm and solution-focused

If no solution is apparent, don't continue to worry and make yourself sick.

If you arrive at a solution, resolve yourself to it and visualize your actions and success.

If you must accept the situation because no change is possible, meditate on acceptance and voluntarily accept this suffering.

Keep in mind that even small problems or episodes can grow when we feed them.

When we face suffering and continually search for causes or the "why" of things, we learn that this pattern can often contribute to more suffering. In this sense, we can gain freedom from suffering by releasing ourselves from this burden. When we recognize that other beings also suffer and are in pain, we can develop compassion for them. This meditation is an effective tool for reinforcing this knowledge.

Developing Compassion for Others

All the problems in the world come from cherishing ourselves. All the goodness and joy in the world come from cherishing others. —*Shanti Diva*

As we have discussed, suffering is an unfortunate, yet unavoidable, aspect of life for all sentient beings. In the Buddhist tradition, meditation on suffering is considered an advanced meditative technique called bodichitta.

Bodhicitta: The term *bodhicitta* in Buddhist tradition means "aspiration to enlightenment." When broken down, *bodhi* means a state of mind that is free of all negativity such as anger, ignorance and attachment. The term *chitta* means "awakening mind," or aspiration for a fully awakened state.

The crucial step toward cultivating bodhicitta in meditation is to develop compassion for others through the practice of "cause and effect" visualization. The foundation for this technique is to begin by developing an affinity for all beings and recognizing, in essence, that all sentient beings are connected. Acknowledging that all living beings, in some way, contribute to our own existence.

In your meditation, for example, think of the farmers, animals, gatherers, shippers, producers, inspectors, retailers, cooks, tailors, etc., who must come together to give us clothing. Cultivating a sense of gratitude for other beings and their kindness, and repaying that kindness, is important in developing bodhicitta. Compassion is enhanced by developing an affectionate love for other beings, much like the love a mother has for her child. As a mother has a heartfelt desire to remove the suffering of her child, the goal in bodhicitta is to cultivate a heartfelt relief of another's suffering. With meditation practice focusing on these elements, post-meditative compassion will begin to extend for longer and longer periods in your day-to-day life.

While developing bodhicitta through your meditation practice, pay special attention to how you can remove the suffering of others. In this vein, we may realize that our own activities, such as anger, bad lifestyles or unhealthy activities, contribute somehow to the suffering of others. Therefore, a change in us often contributes to easing the suffering of others. A major part of this journey begins with overcoming our own self-created negativities. Incorporating these qualities into our lives doesn't come easily. These efforts must be continuous, requiring daily effort and an investment in patience.

Equalizing ourselves with others is part of the process of developing bodhicitta. Equalizing can be achieved through the realization that everyone deserves happiness and has the right to be joyful. Part of equalizing ourselves with others involves a contemplation of the faults of self-cherishing.

In this process, it is important to remember that unconditional love has no agenda and that we must stop blaming. The only thing we have to blame is our own selfishness. Here it is important to distinguish that having your own sense of joy and happiness, or cherishing yourself, is not wrong, but selfishness is.

Despite the negative aspects of experiencing or witnessing suffering throughout our lives, there is a positive side to how we can use suffering to enhance meditation practice and ourselves:

When we face suffering and search for its causes, we learn that our negative thoughts and responses can contribute to the problem. In this sense, we can gain freedom from suffering through compassionate meditation and positive actions.

By meditating on suffering, we may begin to develop ideas on how to alleviate the suffering of others.

We can recognize that other beings suffer and are in pain. By doing this in our meditation and actions, we can develop compassion for all living things.

Meditation on suffering is a powerful opponent to the arrogance and pride that can stifle our personal growth.

By attempting through meditation to understand the suffering of other living things, we develop the capacity to better manage and ease our own suffering.

You can utilize analytical meditation on distress and compassion during those times when you feel you are hurting in life or when you witness hurt in others. This type of suffering is familiar to everyone, and can generate negative feelings and actions. When we are in pain (anger), there is an unnatural tendency to isolate ourselves, become silent, or push others away. This too is unhealthy and a sign of illness.

Meditation Practice

In your meditation practice, instead of focusing on your suffering, begin to visualize the suffering of others throughout the world. Begin to focus on the true suffering and loss experienced by others. In your mind, create a picture of someone's or a group's suffering and the situation surrounding that pain. Try not to detach yourself from this image, but instead attempt to view it from a "mother's perspective." That is true love.

When you begin to see all living things as universally connected, it's easy to conceptualize and identify with their emotions. This technique is a powerful tool and can cultivate strong emotions regarding the suffering in the universe. It is a tool of compassion.

If the suffering you visualize can be solved, try not to fret about the pain but begin to shift your focus on a solution(s). If no solution is apparent, don't continue to worry or make yourself sick. When there is no solution and you continue to struggle for answers, it only worsens the problem. Even small problems or episodes can grow when we feed them energy and make ourselves insane.

If you find no solution, begin to meditate on acceptance while voluntarily accepting suffering and its reality. In many ways, this practice is putting yourself in another's shoes through mindful meditation and visualization.

Various Meditation Practices to Cultivate Bodhicitta:

• Meditate on how the interconnection between all beings and how they give of themselves for our survival.

• Meditate on the greatness of all sentient beings, of life, and of the uniqueness of it all.

• Cultivate a "mother's love" for all beings and develop a sense of thankfulness.

• Meditate on the cause and effect of your actions (anger, selfishness and unhealthy behaviors) on others, especially those you love.

• Utilize analytical meditation to develop solutions for relieving the suffering of others.

• Visualize how your own compassion can relieve the suffering of others and impact them in a positive way.

• Practice equalizing yourself with others by visualizing the joys in life and how all beings deserve to experience joy and happiness.

As anger and negative emotions leach into our thinking, they negatively affect our mood and overall temperament. Therefore, it is important to directly work on the emotions themselves. Meditation practices that address the negative consequences of anger and destructive emotions serve as an antidote for these thoughts. Remember that you can't experience love and hatred at the same time for the same object, so meditate on compassion. Another antidote to anger and destructive emotions is the realization of their empty nature and that you can transform them even before they arise.

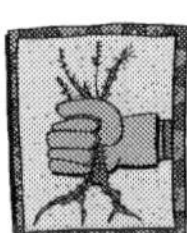 # Chapter 10: Final Thoughts

The solution lies in the understanding of human suffering and making a conscious choice to either contribute to this suffering or become an antidote to it. —Charlie C. Cummins

As we have seen, the foundation for uprooting anger is to pay attention and take responsibility for your emotions and actions.

We have touched on many strategies for not just managing anger, but working toward a goal of uprooting and eliminating it. The journey can be fun and enlightening because freeing yourself from the ills of anger is liberation. When you attend to your thoughts, actions and motives for doing things, you place yourself in a position of being able to free yourself. At this point, you can tune into other people in your life and be an encouraging influence on their lives.

Each day that you can be mindful of not wanting to be influenced by destructive emotions is a day that enhances every moment in life. Without the shackles of anger, life looks brighter, the air smells sweeter, food tastes better and relationships are filled with greater love.

All it takes is the awareness of how destructive anger can be and a routine of strategies that become an integral part of your life. As long as you are awake, you can focus on being present in the moment and committed to the compassionate treatment of yourself and others.

In closing, I look out my window, see the beauty of nature, and hear the laughter of my daughter. I can feel the warmth of my family and know that they are there to support me through the most difficult of times. I understand how anger and destructive emotions can sour all this, and I make a choice each day to do the things I can to dispel these from my life. I choose to do this for myself, but more importantly, for the benefit of other people whose suffering is greater than mine.

I trust that you will join me in this journey, because the result is greater peace for us all.

About the Author

Charlie Cummins, MS, LPC, is a coach, executive advisor, consultant, author and speaker in the area of human performance, with over 20 years experience in helping individuals and organizations. As founder and president of Life Transitions Consulting, he has been featured on CNN, BNN, NBC, and in numerous print articles. As the host of the *Moving toward Greatness* broadcast on Voice America Radio, Charlie focused on strategies for executive coaching and human performance, while incorporating the expertise of leaders from around the world. He offers a unique combination of personal and professional skills gathered from his background in clinical psychology and organizational management. This combination of skills equips him to evaluate and present success principles that help executives and their organizations maximize the use of their number one resource: themselves.

Charlie acquired his master's degree in science from Georgia State University and additional doctoral studies in clinical psychology at Adler School of Psychology in Chicago. Subsequently, he has developed and administered health programs on a national level and has served as a consultant to Fortune 500 companies.

An adventurer whose personal passions include martial arts, skydiving and the outdoors, Charlie is proficient in developing strong, strategic leadership with masterful communication skills. Movement, productivity, organizational insight, the bottom line, and the ability to hire and develop leaders are part of the skill set and experience he offers in a confidential and objective working relationship.

Made in the USA
Charleston, SC
30 August 2016